Basic electrical installation principles

Basic electrical installation principles

Michael Neidle TEng (CEI), FITE, ASEE(Dipl)

*Associate Member of the
Institution of Electrical Engineers*

McGRAW-HILL Book Company (UK) Limited

London · New York · St Louis · San Francisco · Auckland · Bogotá
Guatemala · Hamburg · Johannesburg · Lisbon · Madrid · Mexico
Montreal · New Delhi · Panama · Paris · San Juan · São Paulo · Singapore
Sydney · Tokyo · Toronto

Published by

McGRAW-HILL Book Company (UK) Limited
MAIDENHEAD · BERKSHIRE · ENGLAND

British Library Cataloguing in Publication Data

Neidle, Michael
    Basic electrical installation principles.
    1. Electrical engineering
    I. Title
    621.31'042   TK153   80-40839

    ISBN 0-07-084639-1

12345 JWA 83210

PRINTED AND BOUND IN GREAT BRITAIN

Preface

This book has been written primarily with the aim of assisting students studying for the Part I Certificate of the City and Guilds Electrical Installation Work Course No. 236. It will also be of direct assistance to those taking allied courses with an electrical content or for those who have left their studies behind and require a simple and up-to-date publication for revision purposes.

Since electrical installations are a practical application of electrical engineering, a proper understanding of electrical principles is essential. An example is the common fluorescent fitting where a real grasp of its action and component parts is not possible without a basis of electrical science.

The scope of advancement in the field of electrical installation engineering is extremely wide. Mastery of the book's contents could therefore lay the foundation for a worthwhile career. The author wishes the student the best of luck in his endeavours.

Grateful acknowledgement is given to the following authorities and companies: City & Guilds Institution, British Standards Institution, Chloride Alcad Limited, GEC Machines Limited and Satchwell Sunvic Limited.

Electrical installation symbols (BS 3939)

Switched socket outlet

Socket outlet with interlocking switch

Socket outlet with pilot lamp

Multiple socket outlet example: for 3 plugs

Lighting point or lamp: general symbol note: the number, power and type of the light source should be specified

3×40 W example: three 40 watt lamps

Lamp or lighting point: wall mounted

Emergency (safety) lighting point

Lighting point with built in switch

Heater: type to be specified

Motor: general symbol

Generator: general symbol

Thermostat: block symbol

Switch with pilot lamp

Period limiting switch

Regulating switch eg. dimmer

Push button

Luminous push button

Main control or intake point

Distribution board or point

note: the circuits controlled by the distribution board may be shown by the addition of an appropriate qualifying symbol or reference

examples: heating

lighting

ventilating

Main or sub-main switch

Contactor

Symbol	Description
	Integrating meter
	Starter
	Changeover switch
	Transformer
E	Consumer's earthing terminal
	Earth
	Electrical appliance: general symbol note: if necessary use designations to specify type
	Fan

Symbol	Description
	Single-pole, one-way switch note: number of switches at one point may be indicated
	Two-pole, one-way switch
	Three-pole, one-way switch
	Cord-operated single-pole one-way switch
	Two-way switch
	Intermediate switch
	Time switch
	Socket outlet (mains): general symbol

Symbol	Description
	Single fluorescent lamp
	Group of three fluorescent lamps
3×40 W	example: simplified representation
	Spot light
	Bell
N	Indicator panel N = number of ways
	Telephone point

Conversion factors

$$1 \text{ inch} = 25.4 \text{ mm}$$
$$1 \text{ square inch (in}^2) = 645 \text{ mm}^2$$
$$1 \text{ yd} = 0.9144 \text{ m}$$
$$1 \text{ mm} = 0.03937 \text{ in}$$
$$1 \text{ m} = 39.37 \text{ in}$$
$$= 1.094 \text{ yd}$$
$$= 1000 \ (10^3) \text{ mm}$$
$$1 \text{ square metre (1 m}^2) = 10^6 \text{ mm}^2$$
$$1 \text{ cubic metre (m}^3) = 10^9 \text{ mm}^3$$
$$1 \text{ lb} = 0.4536 \text{ kg}$$
$$1 \text{ litre} = 0.22 \text{ gallons}$$
$$1 \text{ litre of water has a mass of 1 kg}$$
$$1 \text{ megohm (M}\Omega) = 10^6 \ \Omega$$
$$1 \text{ milliamp (mA)} = \frac{1}{10^3} \text{ A}$$
$$= 10^{-3} \text{ A}$$
$$1 \text{ kW} = 10^3 \text{ W}$$
$$1 \text{ kVA} = 10^3 \text{ VA}$$

1. Calculations

We take our present number system for granted but it goes back to the dawn of mankind. Early man found no need for counting. Life was simple: usually animals were killed for food and skins formed simple clothing. Barter or exchange was sufficient for primitive peoples where a skin might be exchanged for an axe

Counting probably started by notches on trees or scratches on stones. With the birth of civilizations, number systems developed (Fig. 1.1). The Roman numerals were a clear advance on earlier systems:

I II III IV V VI VII VIII IX X XV(15) XX(20) XXX(30) etc.

and made for easy adding, but difficulties arise with multiplication and division.

Our present decimal number system is hindu-arabic in origin, being based on ten – probably from ten fingers. Computer operations use the binary system with *two* instead of *ten* for the place position. Whereas in the decimal method 11 is made up of $10+1$ and represents the number eleven, the binary number 11 is equal to three $(2+1)$.

The following notes are mainly intended to serve as a revision of previous school work directed towards the requirements of electrical calculations.

Most of the work could be carried out by electronic calculators. However, a knowledge of the principles as set out helps towards a fuller understanding of our present number system. Further, the student should not be a slave to the calculator and so be unable to solve simple problems if the battery runs out or is mislaid!

1.1 Fractions

If a circle is divided into eight equal parts (Fig. 1.2) then each portion represents an eighth of the whole circle. The word 'eighth' may be put in a fractional form, i.e., $\frac{1}{8}$. Clearly $\frac{2}{8}=\frac{1}{4}$, $\frac{4}{8}=\frac{1}{2}$ and $\frac{6}{8}=\frac{3}{4}$.

In any of these fractions the number above the line is called the *numerator*, while the number below the line is termed *denominator*. The denominator signifies the number of parts into which the whole must be *divided*; the numerator tells how many of these parts must be taken or *multiplied*.

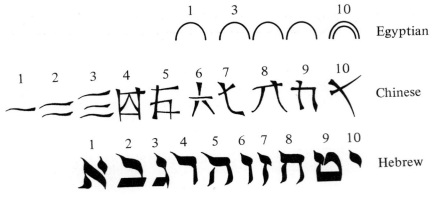

Fig. 1.1   Number systems

EXAMPLE 1.1

At one time stores held 2000 m of conduit. If $\frac{3}{8}$ of this amount was supplied to various contracts, how much conduit was left?

$$\frac{3}{8} \times \frac{\overset{250}{\cancel{2000}}}{1} = 750 \text{ m}$$

$\therefore$ conduit left $= 2000 - 750 = \underline{1250 \text{ m}}$
   or more directly, $\frac{5}{8} \times 2000 = 1250 \text{ m}$

Cancelling simplifies the work. It should be carried out whenever numerator and denominator can be divided by the same number or factor. This cancelling factor should be as large as possible.

EXAMPLE 1.2

Which is bigger, $\frac{8}{9}$ or $\frac{7}{11}$, and by how much?

The lowest common denominator of 9 and 11 must first be found to make the fractions agree to a common basis.

$$\frac{8}{9} = \frac{8 \times 11}{9 \times 11} = \frac{88}{99}$$

$$\frac{7}{11} = \frac{7 \times 9}{11 \times 9} = \frac{63}{99}$$

$$\frac{88}{99} - \frac{63}{99} = \frac{25}{99}$$

$\therefore \frac{8}{9}$ is bigger than $\frac{7}{11}$ by $\frac{25}{99}$

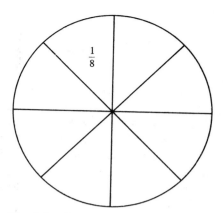

Fig. 1.2 Circle divided into fractions

The common denominator was seen by inspection to be the product of 9 and 11, i.e., 99. This latter number is divided by the denominator of each fraction and then multiplied by the respective numerator. The common denominator is often called the *least common multiple* (LCM) and is the smallest number into which all of the denominators will divide.

Improper fractions is the name given to fractions where the numerator is larger than the denominator. They can always be changed into whole numbers:

$$\frac{23}{5} = 4\frac{3}{5}$$

Dividing the 5 into 23 goes four times with a remainder 3.

The whole number and fraction is termed a *mixed number*. Students learn that with practice, a number of stages in the solution can be worked out mentally, but as always, checking is necessary.

EXAMPLE 1.3

Evaluate: (**a**) $\frac{3}{4} - \frac{1}{12} \times \frac{5}{7} + \frac{1}{2}$ (**b**) $\frac{2}{5} \div (\frac{1}{2} \times \frac{7}{8})$

(**a**) $\dfrac{3}{4} - \dfrac{1}{12} \times \dfrac{5}{7} + \dfrac{1}{2}$

$= \dfrac{3}{4} - \dfrac{5}{84} + \dfrac{1}{2}$

$= \dfrac{63 - 5 + 42}{84}$ (*Note.* Multiplication (or division) must be carried out first.)

$= \dfrac{100}{84}$

$= \dfrac{25}{21} = 1\dfrac{4}{21}$

(b) $\dfrac{2}{5} \div \left(\dfrac{1}{2} \times \dfrac{7}{8}\right)$

$= \dfrac{2}{5} \div \dfrac{7}{16}$

$= \dfrac{2}{5} \times \dfrac{16}{7}$ Multiplying by the reciprocal

$= \dfrac{32}{35}$

EXAMPLE 1.4

A man purchases a total of 144 electric lamps. A quarter are of type A, a third of type B, and the remainder type C. What fraction of the total is type C and what are the actual amounts of each type purchased?

$$\text{Type A} + \text{type B} = \dfrac{1}{4} + \dfrac{1}{3}$$

$$= \dfrac{3+4}{12} = \dfrac{7}{12}$$

$$\text{Remainder} = 1 - \dfrac{7}{12} = \dfrac{5}{12}$$

$$\therefore \text{Type C} = \dfrac{5}{12} \text{ of the total}$$

$$\text{Type A} = \dfrac{1}{4} \times 144 = 36 \text{ lamps}$$

$$\text{Type B} = \dfrac{1}{3} \times 144 = 48 \text{ lamps}$$

$$\text{Type C} = \dfrac{5}{12} \times 144 = 60 \text{ lamps}$$

As a check, $36 + 48 + 60$ $= 144$

1.2 Decimal fractions

The term 'decimal fractions' is usually shortened to the single word 'decimals'. They are simply common fractions which have been calculated from a denominator of 10 (or a multiple of 10). Some useful decimals which should be committed to memory are:

$$\frac{1}{10} = 0.1$$

$$\frac{1}{100} = 0.01$$

$$\frac{1}{1000} = 0.001$$

$$\frac{1}{4} = \frac{25}{100} = 0.25$$

$$\frac{1}{2} = \frac{50}{100} = 0.5$$

$$\frac{3}{4} = \frac{75}{100} = 0.75$$

$$\frac{1}{8} = \frac{125}{1000} = 0.125$$

To convert a fraction into a decimal, the denominator is divided into the numerator.

EXAMPLE 1.5

Convert $\frac{5}{8}$ to a decimal.

$$\frac{5}{8} = \frac{0.625}{8)5.000} = \underline{0.625}$$

EXAMPLE 1.6

(**a**) *A machine is rated as 78.68 kilowatts (kW); what is its power in watts?*
(**b**) *Multiply 36.42 by 4.7*
(**c**) *Calculate* $\dfrac{46.002}{0.7}$ *to three decimal places.*

(**a**) To convert kilowatts to watts multiply by 1000, i.e., shift the decimal point three places to the right. As there are only two figures, a nought must be added.

$$78.68 \, kW = \underline{78\,680 \text{ watts}}$$

(**b**) Ignoring the decimal points,

$$3642 \times 47 = 171\ 174$$

The number of figures after the decimal point is three, so that there must be three decimal places in the answer.

$$36.42 \times 4.7 = \underline{171.174}$$

(**c**) Always turn the divisor into a whole number; here multiplying both sides by ten.

$$\frac{46.002}{0.7} = \frac{460.02}{7}$$

By long division, adding the required number of noughts,

$$\frac{65.7171}{7)460.0200}$$

$$\frac{46.002}{0.7} = \underline{65.717}$$ to three places of decimals

For two decimal places the answer becomes 65.72 following the rule 'if the last digit is 5 or above, then the preceding digit is raised by one'.

1.3 Percentages

Multiplying a fraction or a number by 100 turns it into a percentage. The symbol for 'per cent' is %.

Thus $\frac{5}{8}$ as a percentage is $\frac{5}{8} \times 100 = 0.625\%$

3 as a percentage is $3 \times 100 = 300\%$

0.675 as a percentage is $0.675 \times 100 = 67.5\%$

Conversely, a percentage can be converted into a number when divided by 100:

$$85\% = \frac{85}{100} = 0.85$$

EXAMPLE 1.7

If 10 000 metres of cable have been used for 75 per cent of an installation,

6

what is the amount of cable required for the entire installation?

$$75\% = 10\,000 \text{ m}$$

$$1\% = \frac{10\,000}{75}$$

$$100\% = \frac{10\,000 \times 100}{75} = \underline{13\,333 \text{ metres}}$$

(N.B. 100% represents the total amount of cable required.)

EXAMPLE 1.8

The wholesale price of a motor starter is £50. However, if six or more are purchased, a discount of 20 per cent is allowed. An additional discount of $2\frac{1}{2}$ per cent is given if the account is settled within 28 days. Assuming that the purchaser pays cash, what will be the cost of 12 starters if 10 per cent delivery charge is added to the bill?

Wholesale price of 12 starters $= 12 \times £50 = £600.00$

20% discount $= \dfrac{20}{100} \times £600 = £120.00$

Price less discount $\quad\qquad\qquad\qquad £480.00$

Cash discount $= \dfrac{2\frac{1}{2}}{100} \times £480 = \dfrac{£12.00}{£468.00}$

10% delivery charge $= \dfrac{10}{100} \times £468 = £46.80$

Nett cost $\qquad\qquad\qquad\qquad = \underline{£514.80}$

1.4 Index notation

$$100 = 10 \times 10 \qquad\qquad 10^2 \text{ (spoken as 'ten squared')}$$
$$1000 = 10 \times 10 \times 10 \qquad 10^3 \text{ (spoken as 'ten cubed')}$$
$$10\,000 = 10 \times 10 \times 10 \times 10 \quad 10^4 \text{ (spoken as 'ten to the power of four')}$$
$$1\,000\,000\,000 = \qquad\qquad 10^9 \text{ (spoken as 'ten to the power of nine')}$$

From the above it can be seen that the index shows the amount of noughts after the one and also indicates the number of times ten is multiplied by itself.

$$\frac{1}{10} = \frac{1}{10^1} = 10^{-1} \text{ ('ten to the minus one')}$$

$$\frac{1}{100} = \frac{1}{10^2} = 10^{-2} \text{ ('ten to the minus two')}$$

$$\frac{1}{1000} = \frac{1}{10^3} = 10^{-3} \text{ ('ten to the minus three')}$$

Changing the base and its index from denominator to numerator alters the index sign. The rule also applies where change is made from numerator to denominator.

e.g., $10^4 = \dfrac{1}{10^{-4}}$. To multiply, add indices; to divide, subtract indices.

EXAMPLE 1.9

Evaluate

$$\frac{10^7 \times 10^2 \times 10}{10^6 \times 1000}.$$

$$\frac{10^7 \times 10^2 \times 10}{10^6 \times 1000}$$

$$\frac{10^7 \times 10^2 \times 10^1}{10^6 \times 10^3} = \frac{10^{7+2+1}}{10^{6+3}} = \frac{10^{10}}{10^9} = 10^{10-9} = 10^1 = \underline{10}$$

We are now in a position to understand the meaning of some of the multiples and sub-multiples which are of frequent occurrence in electrical calculations.

$$\text{mega (M)} = 10^6$$
$$\text{kilo (k)} = 10^3$$
$$\text{milli (m)} = 10^{-3}$$
$$\text{micro } (\mu) = 10^{-6}$$

So 100 megawatts (MW) = 10 000 000 = 10^8 W

20.6 kilovolts (kV) = 20 600 V

$$5 \text{ milliamps (mA)} = \frac{5}{1000} \text{A} = 5 \times 10^{-3} \text{ A} = 0.005 \text{ A}$$

$$16 \text{ microhms } (\mu\Omega) = \frac{16}{10\,000\,000}\,\Omega = 16 \times 10^{-6}\,\Omega = 0.000\,016\,\Omega$$

1.5 Squares and square roots

When a number is multiplied by itself the result becomes the square of that number, thus:

$$\text{the square of 2 is } 2 \times 2 = 2^2 = 4$$
$$\text{the square of 20 is } 20 \times 20 = 20^2 = 400$$
$$\text{the square of 0.9 is } 0.9 \times 0.9 = 0.9^2 = 0.81$$

The reverse process produces the square root, so that the square roots of 4, 400, and 0.81 are respectively 2, 20, and 0.9. While the index 2 gives the square of the number, a special sign ($\sqrt{\ }$) is used for square roots. As we have seen, $\sqrt{0.81} = 0.9$.

It is clear that squares are easier to calculate. For square roots we must find a number which when multiplied by itself gives the original number. The square roots of perfect squares, which are whole numbers, can often be obtained mentally. $\sqrt{4}$, $\sqrt{9}$, $\sqrt{16}$, $\sqrt{25}$, $\sqrt{36}$, $\sqrt{49}$, $\sqrt{64}$, $\sqrt{81}$, $\sqrt{100}$, $\sqrt{121}$, $\sqrt{144}$, and $\sqrt{169}$ respectively are 2, 3, 4, 5, 6, 7, 8, 9, 10, 11, 12, and 13. Other numbers may be found by means of square root tables or electronic calculators. Here a warning note may be sounded. While calculators speed calculations, their use should not be at the expense of the student's understanding of the operations involved.

Certain square roots which commonly occur in electrical calculations are worth remembering:

$$\sqrt{2} = 1.414$$
$$\sqrt{3} = 1.732$$
$$\sqrt{10} = 3.16$$

EXAMPLE 1.10

Find the square root of (**a**) 0.1 (**b**) 300

(**a**) $\sqrt{0.1} = \sqrt{\dfrac{1}{10}} = \dfrac{\sqrt{1}}{\sqrt{10}} = \dfrac{1}{3.16} = \underline{0.316}$

Note that the square root of one is equal to one.

(**b**) $\sqrt{300} = \sqrt{3 \times 100} = \sqrt{3} \times \sqrt{100} = 1.732 \times 10 = \underline{17.32}$

1.6 Transposition

To obtain the area of a rectangle, the length is multiplied by the breadth. In algebraic terms, $A = lb$ and A is stated to be the *subject*. By transposing, l or b can be made to be the subject. For this operation you may consider that the equals sign equates or balances the two sides of the equation, so that if a particular quantity multiples or divides *both* sides, then the value of the formula is unchanged. Similarly, if the same value is added or subtracted from both sides, the equation still holds, giving the general rule: 'what is done to one side must be done to the other'.

To make *l* the subject, *b* must be removed from the right-hand side. Dividing both sides by *b*:

$$A = lb$$

then

$$\frac{A}{b} = \frac{lb}{b}$$

by cancelling, $l = A/b$

EXAMPLE 1.11

If $E = V + Ir$ transpose (**a**) *V* (**b**) *r*

(**a**) $E = V + Ir$
   $V = E - Ir$ by subtracting *Ir* from both sides
(**b**) $Ir = E - V$ by subtracting *V* from both sides and
                  adding *Ir* to both sides

   $r = \dfrac{E - V}{I}$ dividing both sides by *I*

1.7 Plane figures

A square is the shape of a particular four-sided figure where all sides are of the same length (*l*). The area (*A*) of the plane surface enclosed by the sides is obtained by

$$A = l^2$$
$$\therefore l = \sqrt{A} \text{ by taking the square root of both sides}$$

EXAMPLE 1.12

A square switchroom has a floor area of 18 square metres, what is the length of one wall?

$$l = \sqrt{A}$$
$$= \sqrt{18}$$
$$= \sqrt{2} \times \sqrt{9}$$
$$= \sqrt{2} \times \sqrt{9}$$
$$= 1.414 \times 3 = \underline{4.242 \text{ m}}$$

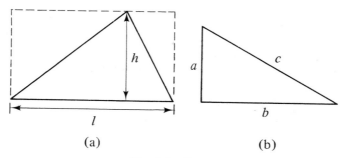

Fig. 1.3 Triangles

The area of a triangle (Fig. 1.3(a)) may be seen as half that of a rectangle, i.e, $lh/2$.

In a right-angled triangle (Fig. 1.3(b)) the longest side is called the hypotenuse. Its length can be calculated by *Pythagoras' theorem*, which was set out more than 2500 years ago and may be stated as: 'in any right-angled triangle the square of the hypotenuse is equal to the sum of the squares of the other two sides'. So that in Fig. 1.3(b),

$$c^2 = \sqrt{a^2 + b^2}$$

taking the square root of both sides,

$$c = \sqrt{a^2 + b^2}$$

EXAMPLE 1.13

A 4-core cable has to be run across two diagonally opposite corners of a small rectangular playground measuring 40 m by 100 m. What is the length of the trench which must be cut to accommodate the cable?

The conditions are illustrated in Fig. 1.4. By Pythagoras' theorem,

$$\text{Length of trench} = \sqrt{40^2 + 100^2}$$
$$= \sqrt{1600 + 10\,000}$$
$$= \sqrt{11\,600}$$
$$= \underline{107.7\ m}$$

In schools the area of a *circle* is usually given as πr^2, where r is the radius and π (pi) equal to $3\frac{1}{7}$ or 3.142. The question arises, what exactly does π represent? In any circle (Fig. 1.5)

$$\pi = \frac{\text{length of circumference}}{\text{diameter}}$$

11

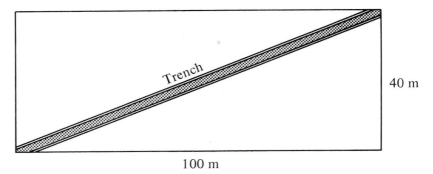

Fig. 1.4

EXAMPLE 1.14

Calculate the circumference of a 20 mm conduit.

With length of circumference c, and diameter d,

$$\pi = \frac{c}{d}$$

By transposition, $C = \pi d$

$$= 3.142 \times 20 = \underline{62.84 \text{ mm}}$$

For convenience, the area equation in terms of the diameter is normally adopted for electrical installation calculations. Since radius is half the

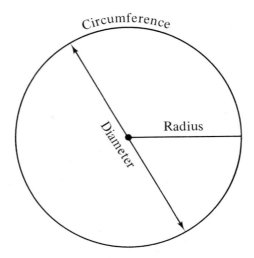

Fig. 1.5   Circle terms

length of the diameter,

$$A = \pi r^2 \qquad (1)$$

$$= \pi \left(\frac{d}{2}\right)^2$$

$$= \pi \frac{d^2}{4}$$

or

$$A = \frac{\pi}{4} d^2 \qquad (2)$$

As π divided by 4 is equal to 0.7854, a third alternative form for determining the area is

$$A = 0.7854 d^2 \qquad (3)$$

EXAMPLE 1.15

A cylindrical transformer tank requires 12 m³ *(cubic metres) of oil to be completely filled. If the height is* 2 m, *calculate* (**a**) *the area of base* (**b**) *the diameter of the tank.*

(**a**) Volume = area of base × height

i.e., $V = Ah$

$$A = \frac{V}{h}$$

$$= \frac{12}{2} = 6 \, m^2$$

$$A = \frac{\pi}{4} d^2$$

(**b**) Also

$$A = 0.7854 d^2$$

$$d^2 = \frac{A}{0.7854}$$

$$d = \sqrt{\frac{A}{0.7854}}$$

$$= \sqrt{\frac{6}{0.7854}} = 2.764 \, m$$

$$A = \pi r^2$$
$$= \pi \left(\frac{d}{2}\right)^2$$
$$= \frac{\pi d^2}{4}$$
$$= 0.7854 d^2$$

1.8 Graphical representation

Graphs are important for showing pictorially the relation between two or more quantities.

13

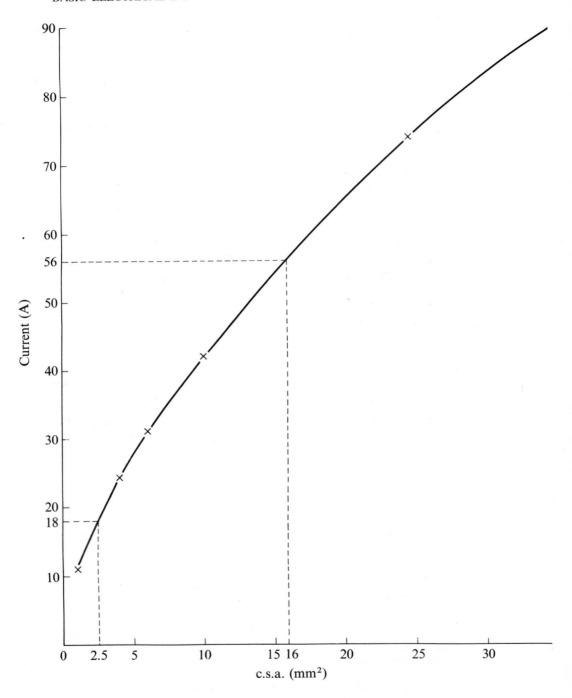

Fig. 1.6   Graph of PVC cables.

EXAMPLE 1.16

An IEE table sets out certain sizes of PVC cables with corresponding current ratings as follows:

Cross-sectional area (mm^2)	1	1.5	4	6	10	25	35
Current rating (amperes	11	13	24	31	42	73	90

Draw an appropriate graph and show what the current rating would be for (a) 2.5 mm^2 cable and (b) the cable size to carry 56 A.

Large scales for the horizontal (*x* axis) and vertical (*y* axis) assist in forming a clear graph. As set out on standard A4 graph paper (Fig. 1.6), 1 mm length is equal to 1 mm^2 of c.s.a. (cross-sectional area) and for the current 1 mm is equal to 1 ampere.

In order to produce the graph, a small cross or circle is placed for each corresponding c.s.a. and current rating value. The points are then joined to form a smooth graph (Fig. 1.6). The required intermediate values are:

   (a) 18 A   (b) 16 mm^2

Block diagrams and bar charts also come under the heading of graphs.

EXAMPLE 1.17

A firm of electrical contractors had the monthly usage (in metres) of 4-core heavy duty MICS cable, over the period of a year as follows:

Jan	Feb	March	April	May	June	July	Aug	Sept	Oct	Nov	Dec
127	334	300	58	426	357	286	87	96	540	525	216

Display the amount used monthly by a bar chart.

The values are shown in Fig. 1.7.

1.9 Exercises

1. Calculate (a) $\frac{1}{2} + \frac{2}{3} + 1\frac{5}{8} - \frac{2}{5}$

            (b) $\frac{3}{4} - \frac{7}{8} + \frac{2}{3} + \frac{1}{6}$

            (c) convert (i) $\frac{7}{8}$ into a decimal number

                  (ii) 0.416 into a fraction

2. What is the value of (a) $\dfrac{1}{10^{-7}}$ (b) $\sqrt{10\,000}$ (c) $10^3 \times 10^7$

    (d) $10^4 \div 10^{-2}$ (e) $\dfrac{2^4 \times 2^3 \times 2^5}{2^7 \times 2}$?

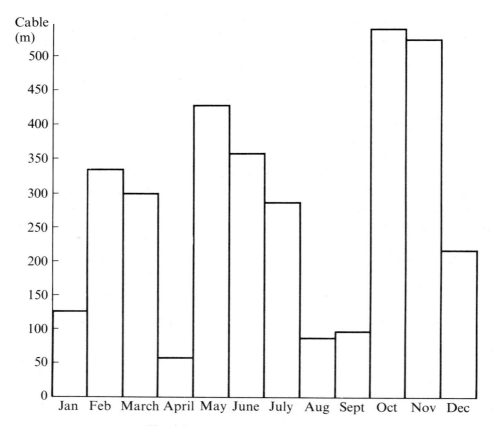

Fig. 1.7 Bar chart of cable installed

3. Make x the subject in each of the following:
    (a) $y = 2x$ (b) $y = \frac{1}{2}x$ (c) $y = x^2$ (d) $y = \sqrt{x}$ (e) $y = x + 2$
    (f) $y = 2x - 2$ (g) $y = \sqrt{a + x}$ (h) $y = 9 + x^2$

4. (a) The wall thickness of a 32 mm conduit is given as 1.8 mm. What are the internal and external diameters of the conduit?

    (b) Which of the following voltages is smallest:
       (i) 0.05 V (ii) 500 μV (iii) 50 mV (iv) 0.005 MV?

5. (a) If $Z = \sqrt{R^2 + X^2}$, calculate the value of X if $Z = 13$ and $R = 5$.

    (b) The value of $R_1 = R_0 (1 + \alpha t)$. If $R_0 = 50$, $\alpha = 0.004$, and $t = 20$, find the value of R_1.

6. The lightning conductor of a building consists of a copper rod of circular section 25 mm diameter by 2.2 m in length. Calculate (a) the volume of the copper rod, and (b) the weight assuming that the density of copper is 8930 kg/m^3.

7. A rectangular water heater is 1 m high with a base 185 mm by 230 mm. Calculate the volume of water in litres when full (1 litre = 10^6 mm^3).

8. The cost of servicing and repairing a control panel is made up as follows:

Rewiring £5.00
Spares provided 26.00
Testing fee 10.00
Commissioning fee 15 min at 8.00 per hour
Labour 4 hours at 6.50 per hour

If Value Added Tax (VAT) of 8 per cent is added to the total bill, calculate the total cost to the customer.

9. A circular conductor of diameter D mm has a cross-sectional area of $\frac{\pi D^2}{4}$ mm^2. If D is doubled its c.s.a. would be:

(a) doubled
(b) 4 times greater
(c) π times greater
(d) π^2 times greater?

10. The following IEE table gives the nominal diameter of copper fuse wires and their respective current ratings:

Nominal diameter of wires (mm)	0.35	0.50	0.60	0.75	1.25	1.53	2.00
Current rating of fuse (A)	10	15	20	25	45	60	100

(a) Produce a smooth curve from these figures.
(b) From the graph find:
  (i) the fuse diameter for a current rating of 80 A;
  (ii) the current rating for a fuse wire of diameter 0.85 mm.

2. Circuit calculations

2.1 The electric current

The 13 A plug is probably the most familiar of all electrical accessories. The plug contains a 3 A or 13 A fuse and the question arises, what exactly is an ampere? It may be defined as the rate of flow of a certain quantity, or charge, of electricity along a conductor. The quantity of electricity is measured in coulombs, so that the current in amperes becomes the coulombs per second.

For an understanding of the coulomb it is necessary to have some knowledge of the fundamental structure of matter. The smallest part of any material is called a molecule. Yet molecules themselves consist of one or more atoms. Water, for example, is made up of H_2O, which means that one molecule of water comprises two atoms of hydrogen and one atom of oxygen.

Finally, these unimaginably small atoms have been found by scientists to be largely electrical in nature. There is a central core containing one or more positive proton charges surrounded by an equal number of spinning planetary negatively charged electrons. Hydrogen is the simplest atom and has but one proton and orbiting electron. The helium atom (Fig. 2.1) consists of two electrons balanced by a positive proton charge of two (Fig. 2.1).

At the other end of the scale, uranium is the heaviest atom, possessing 92 electrons balanced by 92 proton charges.

2.2 Quantity

The coulomb forms the unit for the basic quantity of electricity and consists of 6.3×10^{18} electrons. The familiar ampere is the rate of flow of electricity and is the number of coulombs passing, a particular point in a circuit, per second.

Care is necessary not to confuse symbols with units. The symbol for quantity is Q and that for current I, while the abbreviations for coulomb and ampere are respectively C and A. With t representing time in seconds,

$$I = \frac{Q}{t} \text{ amperes (A)}$$

By transposition, $Q = It$ coulombs (C)

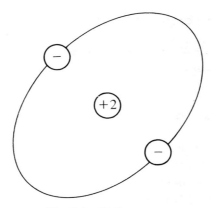

Fig. 2.1   Helium atom

EXAMPLE 2.1

(**a**) *If* 3000 *coulombs pass through a circuit in* 5 *minutes, what is the current flowing?*

(**b**) *A current of* 13 *amperes is maintained for* 1 *hour, how many coulombs pass through the circuit during this period?*

(**a**) $I = \dfrac{Q}{t} = \dfrac{3000}{5 \times 60} = \underline{10 \text{ A}}$

(**b**) $Q = It = 13 \times 60 \times 60 = \underline{46\,800 \text{ C}}$

A larger unit which is often used in practice is the ampere-hour (Ah), the quantity of electricity passing through a circuit if a current of 1 A is maintained for 1 hour, so that an alternative answer to part (b) above would be 13 Ah. Car batteries and secondary cells require charging in ampere-hours.

The range of current values is exceedingly wide: from microamperes (μA) required for certain electronic apparatus to the thousands of amperes (kA) passing through the national grid transmission lines.

2.3   Voltage and resistance

In order for current to flow there must be an electromotive force (e.m.f.), as the source, or potential difference (p.d.) between two points of the circuit. As an analogy, water flows through a pipe when there is a pressure difference caused by a difference in level.

The p.d. is measured in volts and V often stands for both the unit and symbol. Typical voltages are 3 V for a torch lamp, constructional sites 110 V (55 V to earth), substations 11 kV.

All conductors offer some resistance to the flow of electric current. The unit of resistance is the ohm (Ω) and its actual value depends on four factors, namely type of material, length, cross-sectional area (c.s.a.), and temperature.

The longer the conductor, the greater is its resistance, so that resistance is proportional to conductor length. On the other hand, a thicker wire permits an easier flow of electric current, so that the resistance varies inversely as the c.s.a.

EXAMPLE 2.2

A 50 metre conductor with a c.s.a. of 2.5 mm² has a resistance of 0.03 Ω. If it is to be replaced by a similar material 30 m long and of c.s.a. 1.0 mm², what is the resistance of the replacement?

$$\text{Resistance of new conductor original resistance} \times \frac{\text{ratio of lengths}}{\text{ratio of c.s.a.}}$$

$$= 0.03 \times \frac{30/50}{1.0/2.5}$$

$$= \frac{0.03 \times 30 \times 2.5}{50 \times 1.0} = \underline{0.045 \ \Omega}$$

2.4 Ohm's law

Circuit calculations are based on the method as set out by Dr G. S. Ohm more than 150 years ago. They show the relationship between current, voltage and resistance.

$$I = \frac{V}{R} \qquad \text{where } I \text{ is in amperes}$$

By transposition,

$$V = IR \qquad V \text{ in volts}$$

$$R = \frac{V}{I} \qquad R \text{ in ohms}$$

The triangle may serve as a memory aid for Ohm's law. Covering the symbol required, it is then given by the other two letters.

EXAMPLE 2.3

(**a**) *The element of an electric kettle when hot is 75 Ω. If it is plugged into a 240 V circuit, what is the current taken by the element?*

(**b**) *A current of 0.001 A passes through a resistor of value 45 ohms. Calculate the voltage across the ends of the resistor.*

(**c**) *If a certain equipment is rated at 24 V and requires operation by a current of 20 μA, what is its resistance?*

Draw the circuits and set out the values as given in each case.

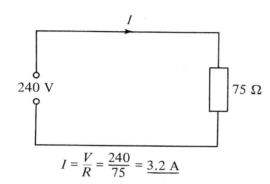

$$I = \frac{V}{R} = \frac{240}{75} = \underline{3.2\ A}$$

Fig. 2.2(a)   Ohm's law calculations

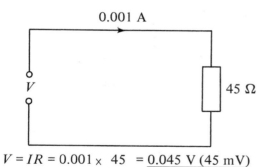

$$V = IR = 0.001 \times 45 = \underline{0.045\ V}\ (45\ mV)$$

Fig. 2.2(b)

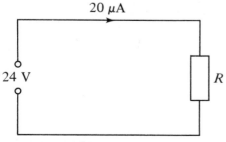

$$R = \frac{V}{I} = \frac{24 \times 10^6}{20} = 1\ 200\ 000\ \Omega = \underline{1.2\ M\ \Omega}$$

Fig. 2.2(c)

2.5   Series circuits

Resistors are stated to be in series when they are connected together as links in a chain (Fig. 2.3). The same current I passes through each resistor and the supply voltage V is equal to the sum of the voltage across each resistor so that $V = V_1 + V_2$.

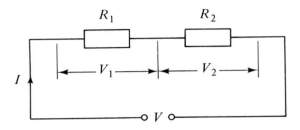

Fig. 2.3   Resistors in series

Applying Ohm's law,

$$V_1 = IR_1$$
$$V_2 = IR_2$$

If R is equal to the value of the combined resistance,

$$IR = IR_1 + IR_2$$
$$= I(R_1 + R_2)$$

and

$$R = R_1 + R_2$$

EXAMPLE 2.4

From the circuit diagram in Fig. 2.4 calculate (**a**) R_x (**b**) V_1 *and* V_2

(**a**) Total resistance $R = \dfrac{\text{Total voltage } (V)}{\text{current } (I)}$

$$= \frac{240}{5} = \underline{48\ \Omega}$$

Also $R = 8 + R_x$

Therefore $48 = 8 + R_x$

$$R_x = 48 - 8 = \underline{40\ \Omega}$$

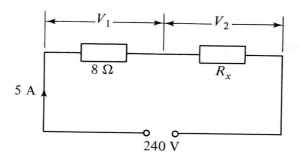

Fig. 2.4

(b)

$$V_1 = IR_1$$
$$= 5 \times 8 = \underline{40 \text{ V}}$$
$$V_2 = IR_x$$
$$= 5 \times 40 = \underline{200 \text{ V}}$$

As a check it will be seen that

$$V = V_1 + V_2 = 240 \text{ V}$$

2.6 Parallel circuits

These are fundamentally different from the series arrangement. Referring to Fig. 2.5 it will be seen that the same voltage V is across each resistor and that $I = I_1 + I_2 + I_3$.

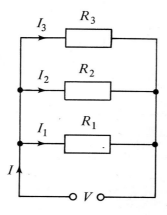

Fig. 2.5   Parallel circuit

Applying Ohm's law to each resistor,

$$I_1 = \frac{V}{R_1}$$

$$I_2 = \frac{V}{R_2}$$

$$I_3 = \frac{V}{R_3}$$

Also

$$I = \frac{V}{R}$$ where R is the equivalent resistance of the parallel connected resistors

Therefore

$$\frac{V}{R} = \frac{V}{R_1} + \frac{V}{R_2} + \frac{V}{R_3}$$

Dividing throughout by V,

$$\frac{1}{R} = \frac{1}{R_1} + \frac{1}{R_2} + \frac{1}{R_3}$$

So for a parallel circuit, the reciprocal of the equivalent resistance is equal to the sum of the reciprocals of the individual resistors.

For circuits containing only two resistors in parallel, some simplification can be made.

$$\frac{1}{R} = \frac{1}{R_1} + \frac{1}{R_2}$$

$$\frac{1}{R} = \frac{R_2 + R_1}{R_1 R_2}$$

By inversion,

$$R = \frac{R_1 R_2}{R_1 + R_2}$$

which in words may be stated as 'the equivalent resistance of two resistors in parallel is equal to their product divided by their sum'.

The equivalent resistance of two resistors in parallel may also be obtained graphically. Figure 2.6 shows the construction for 6 Ω and 3 Ω resistors. A vertical line is scaled to represent 6 ohms, at the foot of which

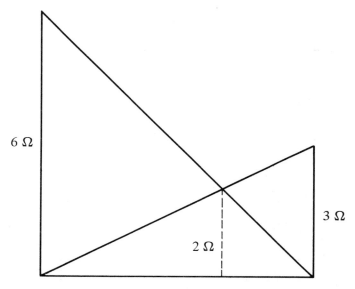

Fig. 2.6   Graphical solution of two resistors in parallel

a horizontal line of convenient length is drawn. At the end a further vertical line is set out to represent 3 ohms to the same scale. The height of the intersection as shown gives the equivalent resistance.

The solution of many circuit problems can be facilitated by changing 'the words into a picture', i.e., extracting the maximum information from the question and putting into a circuit diagram, thus enabling the student to concentrate on obtaining the desired information with the minimum of effort.

EXAMPLE 2.5

A resistor of 10 Ω *is connected in parallel with another of* 15 Ω. *If the supply is* 110 V, *calculate*:
(a) *the equivalent value of both resistors*
(b) *the total current*
(c) *the current through each resistor*

The values are shown in the circuit diagram of Fig. 2.7.

(a) Equivalent resistance $R = \dfrac{R_1 R_2}{R_1 + R_2}$

$$= \frac{10 \times 15}{10 + 15} = \underline{6\ \Omega}$$

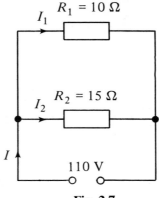

Fig. 2.7

(b) Total current $I = \dfrac{V}{R}$

$$= \dfrac{110}{6} = \underline{18.3\ \text{A}}$$

(c) $I_1 = \dfrac{V}{R_1} = \dfrac{110}{10} = \underline{11\ \text{A}}$

$I_2 = \dfrac{V}{R_2} = \dfrac{110}{5} = \underline{7.3\ \text{A}}$

The combined resistance of two equal resistors in parallel becomes half that of one resistor. Thus the equivalent resistance of 12 Ω and 12 Ω in parallel is 6 Ω. This leads to a general formula of R/n for obtaining the resistance of any number of equal resistors in parallel, where R is the resistance of one resistor and n the number of parallel resistors. The resistance of twelve resistors each of 6 Ω when in parallel becomes 6/12, i.e., 0.5 Ω.

2.7 Series–parallel circuits

These circuits combine the series and parallel arrangements. For total resistance, calculate parallel group(s) and then add the series resistor(s) (Fig. 2.8).

EXAMPLE 2.6

Assuming R_1, R_2 and R_3 in the circuit of Fig. 2.8 are each 6 Ω and R_4 equals 8 Ω. If the voltage across the parallel group is 120 V, calculate:
(a) supply voltage V
(b) current through each resistor I_1, I_2, and I_3.

26

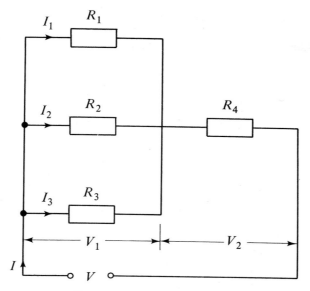

Fig. 2.8   Series–parallel group

(**a**) Equivalent resistance of parallel group $= \frac{6}{3} = 2\,\Omega$ $\left(\text{This can be checked}\right.$

by the reciprocal formula $\dfrac{1}{R} \times \dfrac{1}{R_1} + \dfrac{1}{R_2} + \dfrac{1}{R_3}.\Big)$

$$\text{Total current} = \frac{\text{voltage across parallel group}}{\text{parallel group resistance}} = \frac{120}{2} = 60 \text{ A}$$

This is also the current through R_4.

$$\therefore \text{voltage across } R_4 = I \times R_4 \;\; = \;\; 60 \times 8 \;\; = 480 \text{ V}$$

$$\therefore \text{supply voltage } V = V_1 + V_2 = 120 + 480 = \underline{600 \text{ V}}$$

(**b**) Since total current divides equally into the parallel group, current through I_1, I_2, and I_3 are each $\frac{60}{3} = \underline{20 \text{ A}}$

2.8   Power

The unit of power is the *watt* and is the power dissipated or used up in a resistor having a p.d. of 1 volt across the resistor ends when the current is 1 amp.

$$\text{Power (watts)} = \text{p.d. (volts)} \times \text{current (amperes)}$$

So that

$$P = VI \text{ watts} \tag{1}$$

By means of Ohm's law, two other forms can be obtained:

$$P = (IR)I$$
$$= I^2 R \qquad (2)$$

$$P = V\left(\frac{V}{R}\right)$$

$$= \frac{V^2}{R} \qquad (3)$$

EXAMPLE 2.7

An installation consists of twenty-four 80 W lamps, a 6 kW cooker, six 150 W fans, and a 200 W boiler. Assuming a supply voltage of 240 V, calculate the maximum current.

Maximum current occurs when all loads are switched on together.

$$
\begin{aligned}
24 \times 80 \text{ W lamps} &= 1920 \text{ W} \\
1 \times 6 \text{ kW } \text{ cooker} &= 6000 \text{ W} \\
6 \times 150 \text{ W fans} &= 900 \text{ W} \\
1 \times 200 \text{ W boiler} &= \underline{200 \text{ W}} \\
& 9020 \text{ W}
\end{aligned}
$$

$$
\begin{aligned}
I &= \frac{P}{V} \\
&= \frac{9020}{240} = \underline{37.6 \text{ A}}
\end{aligned}
$$

2.9 Energy

Electrical power may be defined as the *rate* of using up or dissipating energy. The symbol for energy is W with a basic unit of the joule (J), from which it follows:

$$P = \frac{W}{t} \text{ watts, with } t \text{ in seconds}$$

and

$$W = Pt \text{ joules}$$

Similar to the coulomb as the basic unit of quantity, a larger unit for energy, the kilowatt-hour (kWh), is commonly employed in practice. Since

60×60 sec make an hour,

$$1 \, kWh = 1000 \times 60 \times 60$$
$$= 3.6 \times 10^6 \, J$$
$$= 3.6 \, MJ$$

EXAMPLE 2.8

(**a**) *Find the power necessary to absorb* 12 000 J *in* 20 *minutes.*

(**b**) *A* 3 kW *immersion heater is controlled by a time-switch which puts the heater in circuit from* 7 am to 9 am and 4.30 pm to 7 pm. *Calculate the energy consumed daily in* (i) kWh, (ii) joules.

(**a**) $P = \dfrac{W}{t}$

$= \dfrac{12\,000}{20 \times 60} = \underline{10 \, W}$

(**b**) (i) $W = Pt$
$= 3(2 + 2.5) = \underline{13.5 \, kWh}$

(ii) or $W = 13.5 \times 3.6 \times 10^6 = \underline{48.6 \, MJ}$
(since $1 \, kWh = 3.6 \times 10^6 \, J$)

2.10 Costing the use of electricity

Here a kilowatt-hour is referred to as a 'unit' and forms the basis of electricity charges.

EXAMPLE 2.9

A lighting installation consists of twenty 80 W *lamps, twelve* 15 W *lamps, and six* 100 W *lamps. Assuming the entire load is switched on simultaneously, calculate the cost of energy for* 1 *hour at* 2.15p *per* kWh.

$$\text{Total load} = \frac{(20 \times 80) + (12 \times 15) + (6 \times 100)}{1000} = 2.38 \, kW$$

$$\text{Cost of energy per hour} = 2.38 \times 2.15 = \underline{5p}$$

2.11 Resistivity

Conductor resistance is proportional to length (l) and inversely proportional to cross-sectional area (a). Resistance is built up from the resistance

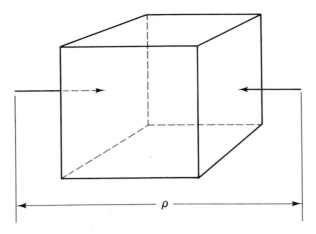

Fig. 2.9 Resistivity

between two opposite faces of a unit cube of the conductor material (Fig. 2.9) of sides 1 m or 1 mm.

The symbol for resistivity is the Greek letter ρ (rho) and the conductor resistance then becomes equal to $\rho \dfrac{1}{a}$. In examination papers and books, the value for resistivity is expressed in various ways:

(a) Ωm (ohm-metre)
(b) $\mu\Omega$m (microhm-metre)
(c) $\mu\Omega$mm (microhm-millimetre)
It is essential to note that for
(a) length must be in metres and c.s.a. in m^2;
(b) as (a) with 10^6 as a divisor to change to ohms;
(c) length in mm, c.s.a. in mm^2, and 10^6 acts as a divisor to change to ohms.

Representative values for resistivity (ρ)			
	Ωm	$\mu\Omega$m	$\mu\Omega$mm
Copper	1.78×10^{-6}	0.0178	17.8
Aluminium	2.7×10^{-6}	0.027	27.0
Brass	7.2×10^{-6}	0.072	72.0
Tungsten	5.3×10^{-6}	0.053	53.0
Iron	9.0×10^{-6}	0.09	90.0

EXAMPLE 2.10

What is the resistance of a copper conductor with a resistivity of 17.8 μΩmm, length 40 m and cross-sectional area 2.5 mm²?

$$\text{Resistance} = \frac{\text{resistivity} \times \text{length}}{\text{c.s.a.}}$$

$$= \rho\frac{1}{a}$$

$$= \frac{17.8 \times 40 \times 10^3}{10^6 \times 2.5} = \underline{0.28 \ \Omega}$$

2.12 Exercises

1. (a) If a current of 1 mA flows in a circuit for 0.5 h, calculate the quantity in coulombs.
   (b) Determine the resistance of a 240 V, 60 W lamp.
   (c) A circuit consists of 40 resistors in parallel, each taking a current of 0.25 A when supplied at 240 V. If the resistors are switched on for half an hour, calculate
   (i) the energy consumed in kWh;
   (ii) the cost if energy is charged at 2.5p per unit.

2. Two 240 V lamps of 100 W and 150 W are connected in parallel to a 240 V supply.
(a) Find the current taken by each lamp.
(b) If the two lamps are connected in series across the supply, what would be the current in the circuit and the potential drops. Assume that the resistance remains the same as in part (a).

3. The power expended in a certain resistor is given by I^2R. If the power expended in a certain resistor is 175 W when the current is 5 A, calculate the power in resistor when:
(a) both current and resistance are doubled;
(b) current is halved and resistance doubled;
(c) current is doubled and resistance is halved.

4. Two resistors A and B are connected in parallel to a 240 V supply. If the power dissipated in A is 1800 W and the power in B is 1080 W, calculate the separate resistances of A and B.

5. A domestic installation comprises the following:

1×10 kW	electric cooker
1×750 W	electric kettle
1×1500 W	washing machine
1×950 W	electric iron
6×100 W	lamps
4×150 W	lamps

Assuming that every piece takes its full load simultaneously, calculate:
(a) the current taken from a 240 V supply;
(b) the cost of energy per hour at 1.95p per unit.
6.

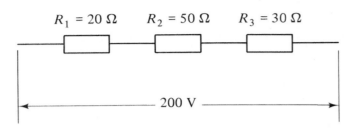

$R_1 = 20\ \Omega$ $R_2 = 50\ \Omega$ $R_3 = 30\ \Omega$

200 V

Fig. 2.10

For the circuit of Fig. 2.10, calculate:
(a) total resistance
(b) current
(c) voltage across R_2
(d) power in R_1
(e) total power of the circuit
7. For the circuit of Fig. 2.11, determine
(a) current passing through load A;
(b) resistance of each of the loads A and B;
(c) power consumed by load B;
(d) total current supply.

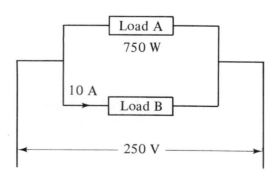

Load A
750 W

10 A

Load B

250 V

Fig. 2.11

8. A twin cable of length 180 m has a cross-sectional area 40 mm²;
calculate the total conductor resistance if the resistivity is $0.017\ \mu\Omega$m.
9. (a) State the relationship between power and energy.
   (b) Given $P = VI$, derive the other two forms for power.

10. (a) Define the 'coulomb' in terms of current and time.
    (b) A 240 V supply delivers 9000 coulombs in half an hour.
        Calculate:
 (i) the current to the circuit;
 (ii) the resistance of the load;
(iii) the load in kW;
(iv) the cost of running the load for 10 h at 2p per kWh.

3. Electromagnetism and electrostatics

3.1 Magnetic fields

We will first investigate the magnetic field as produced by a simple permanent bar magnet. The presence of the field can be shown by laying a sheet of white paper over the magnet and sprinkling iron filings on the part of the sheet covering the magnet. By tapping the sheet, a distinct pattern of the magnetic field is displayed.

In addition, fields have a definite direction which may be shown by the aid of a compass needle. Compasses themselves are miniature magnets with a distinct marking, black or blue, given to the north pole.

Electrical engineers universally agree that *the direction of the field at any point is given by the direction of the north pole when placed in the field at that position*. The needle also provides an alternative method of tracing out the field by 'lines of force' (Fig. 3.1). It is instructive to map out the field of two magnets with adjacent like and adjacent unlike poles (Fig. 3.2).

The field between the north and south poles appear to behave as stretched elastic lines, so that if free to move there would be a force of attraction between the N and S ends of the magnets. With like poles the movement is one of repulsion, since lines of force in the same direction tend to repel each other. This fundamental property of being able to produce a force of movement makes for the production of a vast variety of electrical apparatus; some examples are the motor, circuit-breaker, and a host of household electrical equipment.

3.2 Magnetic materials

Practical magnets may be made by inserting a specimen in a coil through which a heavy direct current is passed. Magnetic materials are termed *ferromagnetic* when consisting of iron, steel, or magnetic alloys. In the ALNICO series, modern magnets often combine the iron with nickel, cobalt, copper, or tungsten in order to obtain superior characteristics of permanent magnets.

Research work is continuous. As a contrast to these traditional ferromagnetic series, ceramic magnets have been produced for specialized electronic equipment and computer 'memories'. A recent development is

34

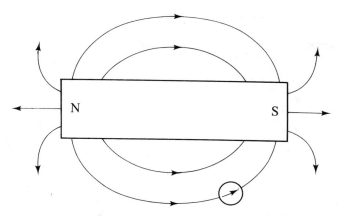

Fig. 3.1 Tracing magnetic lines of force by a compass

the manufacture of rubber-based bonded types permitting flexibility of movement.

3.3 Electromagnetism

Electricity and magnetism are closely tied. Current flowing through a conductor invariably produces a magnetic field in the form of circular or

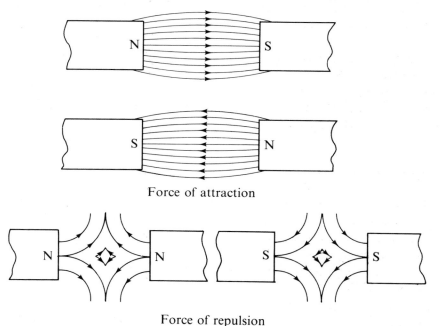

Force of attraction

Force of repulsion

Fig. 3.2 Fields as set up by unlike and like poles

35

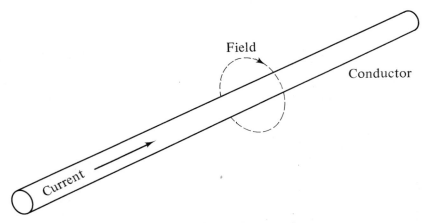

Fig. 3.3 The corkscrew rule

concencentric lines round the wire. There is also a strict relation between the current and field directions often referred to as the *corkscrew rule* (Fig. 3.3).

Winding into a solenoid makes for a stronger magnetic effect and results in a field similar to a bar magnet with a north and south pole at each end (Fig. 3.4). Polarity depends upon which way the current is flowing.

Memory aids for the connection between current and field direction are: (a) the grip following the current direction with rule. By slightly closing the fingers of the right hand so as to follow the direction of the current (Fig. 3.4) then the outstretched thumb points to the north pole; (b) looking at the solenoid end from the left-hand side, the current flows in an anti-clockwise direction to form an   N   for the north pole. Clockwise current direction from the other end shows an   S   for the south pole.

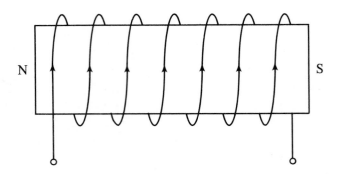

Fig. 3.4 Solenoid

3.4 Magnetic induction

Bringing a soft-iron bar near to the end of a permanent magnet or solenoid makes the bar behave as a permanent magnet with the poles as indicated in Fig. 3.5. Rotating the bar through 180° will produce reversed polarities. The phenomenon is temporary as the soft iron will lose its magnetism when taken away from the magnetic influence.

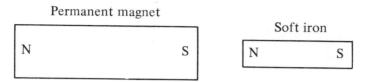

Fig. 3.5   Magnetic induction

3.5 Relays

Due to induction, the soft iron, if free to move, will be attracted to the magnet. The design of relays is based on this action. Figure 3.6 shows the circuit of a simple relay for the purpose of reducing the voltage drop to a bell operated from a long distance and so make for more efficient operation. *Armature* is the name given to the soft-iron piece which is attracted to the solenoid by induced magnetism. In this way, the contacts meet to complete the local bell circuit. This form of relay – often referred to as the telephone type – can be constructed to complete ingenious ON and OFF circuits as may be required for alarms and other systems.

Magnetic fields show a preference for iron, steel, and certain alloys. Air may be considered as possessing a high resistance (the term *reluctance* is

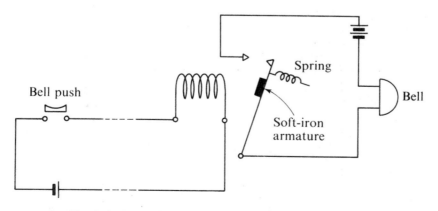

Fig. 3.6   Relay for operating bell at a long distance

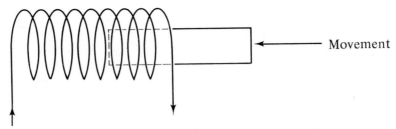

Fig. 3.7 Iron plunger pulled into a solenoid

used in magnetism) to the setting up of a magnetic field. With current flowing through an air-cored solenoid, an iron plunger – suitably placed and free to move – would be pulled into the interior of the solenoid (Fig. 3.7).

The 'sucking' motion would take place irrespective of the current direction, the iron being pulled in by the magnetic force within the coil. This arrangement is an essential part of the contactor type relay and is fitted to many motor starters (Fig. 3.8). Tracing out the circuit reveals that the bridging of the right-hand set of contacts maintains the supply to the motor even when the start button is released.

3.6 Force on a conductor

Current entering a conductor is represented by a cross within a circle, which might be considered as an arrow-head. By the corkscrew rule the

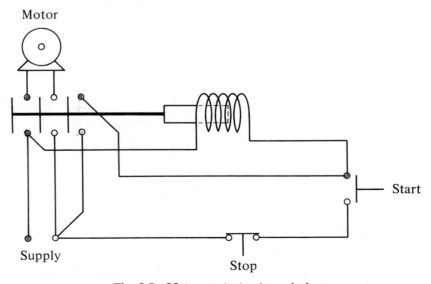

Fig. 3.8 Motor contactor-type starter

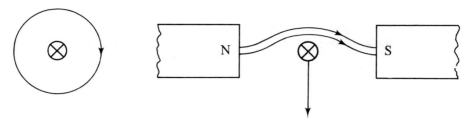

Fig. 3.9 (a) Current and field directions. (b) Resultant fields producing force on a conductor

current and field directions are depicted as in Fig. 3.9(a). Placing this conductor in a field from N and S poles, the two fields combine (Fig. 3.9(b)). There is a strengthening above the conductor, as here they are both in the same direction. Opposite-direction fields result in a weakening field below the conductor. Since magnetic fields behave as stretched elastic lines the conductor will experience downward force. With reversal of current direction or of the north and south poles, the movement would be upwards.

Actual mechanical force is proportional to:

(a) strength of magnetic field (B)

(b) magnitude of current (I)

(c) length of conductor (l)

The product gives the force on the conductor:

$$F = BIl \text{ newtons}$$

where B is in tesla
I in amperes
l in metres

EXAMPLE 3.1

A cable 2.5 m long lies at right angles to a magnetic field of strength 5 teslas. Calculate the force on the conductor when it carries 37 A.

$$F = BIl$$
$$= 5 \times 37 \times 2.5$$
$$= \underline{462.5 \text{ newtons}}$$

3.7 Motor effect

Considering a single looped conductor, Fig. 3.10 depicts how rotary action takes place. It will be noted that current leaving a conductor is shown by a

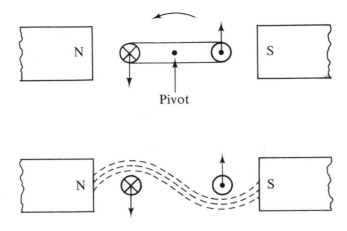

Fig. 3.10 Motor action.

dot within a circle, seen as the point of an arrow. Students should reason out how the fields make for a turning movement in an anti-clockwise direction. Again reversal of current or field results in a change to clockwise rotation.

3.8 Generation of an e.m.f.

Motors may be understood as apparatus for converting electrical energy into mechanical energy. The reverse is also true and mechanical energy can be utilized to generate electrical energy.

Michael Faraday more than 100 years ago discovered that an e.m.f. is generated in a conductor which 'cuts' (crosses) a magnetic field. In principle, motors and generators are similar in construction. As the loop is rotated externally, each side crosses the north and south pole in turn. The purpose of the 2-part commutator (Fig. 3.11) enables current to flow in one direction (direct current or d.c.) externally. Carbon brushes make contact with the rotating commutator.

In practice, the commutator consists of many segments and a large number of loops are connected to form an armature winding.

3.9 Inductance

An e.m.f. may also be generated in a stationary conductor when cut by a varying magnetic field. The effect is known as *inductance*. All conductors are inductive to some extent. Connection to a supply by switching on

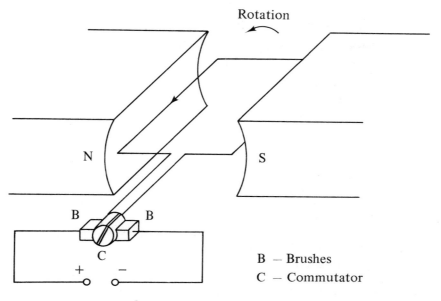

Fig. 3.11 Elementary d.c. generator

causes a rise in current from zero to the load value. The current increase is accompanied by a rise in the magnetic flux thereby cutting the conductor to generate a voltage, and the magnitude is augmented by winding into a coil or solenoid. The value of this induced e.m.f. is proportional to the rate of change of current, i.e., the speed of the current change.

Fluorescent fittings contain a 'choke' consisting of an inductive coil as part of the internal circuit. The starter lamp is designed to produce an extremely rapid rate of current change, thereby causing a sufficiently high voltage to 'strike the arc' across the ends of the tube for starting purposes.

3.10 The capacitor

Quantity of electricity is represented by a charge measured in coulombs. Charges can be stored on two adjacent conducting surfaces insulated from each other by a *dielectric*. Capacitors store these electrostatic charges and are shown on circuit diagrams by two vertical lines slightly apart.

A simple circuit for charging and discharging capacitors is set out in Fig. 3.12. As the 2-way switch makes contact with b from the *off* position, a momentary current flows and a charge is stored on each of the capacitor plates with polarities as shown. At the same time a p.d. exists between the

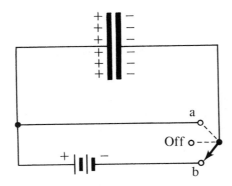

Fig. 3.12 Capacitor charge and discharge circuit

plates. If the switch is moved back to the *off* position, the plates do not lose their charge, indicating that the charge has been stored.

Discharge occurs when the switch has been moved over to position a. The discharge takes place because the p.d. causes a current to flow from one plate to the other. No current actually goes through the dielectric. The current movement is more in the nature of an oscillation (to and fro movement) than a continuous flow.

3.11 Capacitor types

Variations very much depend upon the dielectric medium. Early models consisted of rigid aluminium plates mounted on a spindle with spacing. By turning a knob, variations in areas between two sets of plates permitted changes in capacitance.

Paper capacitors are now in common use, consisting of metal foil and waxed paper tightly coiled together for a large area within the minimum of space. The foil and paper are often immersed in insulating oil. Alternatively, the paper may be metallized by a fine film of metal and fitted into a sealed container.

Mica sheets installed with a silver coating have the advantage of being able to withstand higher voltages.

3.12 Units

Capacitance is the term used to store a charge, and is measured in *farads* (F). A capacitor possesses a capacitance of 1 farad where an applied p.d. of 1 volt is capable of storing 1 coulomb. This leads to the equation capacitance

$$C = \frac{Q}{V} \text{ farads} \qquad \text{where } Q \text{ is in coulombs}$$
$$V \text{ in volts}$$

It may be easier to remember $Q = VC$

Normally the farad is considered too large a unit and is often replaced by the microfarad (μF), equal to a millionth part of a farad. For smaller capacitors there is the picofarad (10^{-12} F) or $\mu\mu$F.

EXAMPLE 3.2

(a) *If a 10 μF capacitor is connected to a 240 V supply, what is the charged stored on the capacitor plates?*

(b) *A certain capacitor produces a p.d. of 125 V between the plates by a charge of 75 μC; what is the capacitance of the capacitor?*

(a) $Q = VC$
$$= 240 \times 10 \times 10^{-6} = \underline{2400 \ \mu C}$$

(b) $Q = VC$

$$C = \frac{Q}{V}$$

$$= \frac{75 \times 10^{-6}}{125} = \underline{0.6 \ \mu F}$$

3.13 Capacitors in series

With capacitors connected in this manner (Fig. 3.13), the same quantity of electricity is stored on each capacitor plate (compare this with resistors connected in series, where the current is the same in all parts of the circuit).

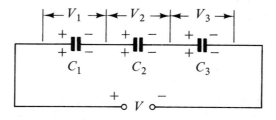

Fig. 3.13 Capacitors in series

The supply voltage is equal to the sum of the voltages across each capacitor:

$$V = V_1 + V_2 + V_3$$

and since $V = Q/C$,

$$\frac{Q}{C} = \frac{Q}{C_1} + \frac{Q}{C_2} + \frac{Q}{C_3}$$

Dividing throughout by Q,

$$\frac{1}{C} = \frac{1}{C_1} + \frac{1}{C_2} + \frac{1}{C_3}$$

which leads to the rule that for *capacitors connected in series, the reciprocal of the equivalent capacitance is equal to the sum of the reciprocal of the capacitances.*

EXAMPLE 3.3

(a) *A circuit consists of four capacitors, 2 μF, 4 μF, 6 μF, 8 μF, connected in series. What is the value of the equivalent capacitance?*

(b) *With a supply voltage of 100 V, calculate the p.d. across each capacitor.*

(a) $\dfrac{1}{C} = \dfrac{1}{C_1} + \dfrac{1}{C_2} + \dfrac{1}{C_3} + \dfrac{1}{C_4}$

$$= \frac{1}{2} + \frac{1}{4} + \frac{1}{6} + \frac{1}{8}$$

$$= \frac{12 + 6 + 4 + 3}{24} = \frac{25}{24}$$

Equivalent capacitance $C = \dfrac{24}{25} = \underline{0.96\ \mu F}$

(b) $Q = VC$

$$= 100 \times 0.96 = 96\ \mu C$$

$$V_1 = \frac{Q}{C_1} \qquad = \frac{96 \times 10^6}{2 \times 10^6} = \underline{48\ V}$$

$$V_2 = \frac{Q}{C_2} \qquad = \frac{96 \times 10^6}{4 \times 10^6} = \underline{24\ V}$$

$$V_3 = \frac{Q}{C_3} \qquad = \frac{96 \times 10^6}{6 \times 10^6} = \underline{16\ V}$$

$$V_4 = \frac{Q}{C_4} \qquad = \frac{96 \times 10^6}{8 \times 10^6} = \underline{12\ V}$$

As a check, it will be seen that the sum of the individual voltages is 100 V.

3.14 Capacitors in parallel

Here the same voltage occurs across each capacitor (Fig. 3.14) so that

$$\text{Charge on capacitor } 1 = Q_1 = VC_1$$

$$\text{Charge on capacitor } 2 = Q_2 = VC_2$$

$$\text{Total charge } Q = VC \text{ where } C \text{ is the total capacitance}$$

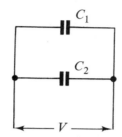

Fig. 3.14   Capacitors in parallel

Also

$$Q = Q_1 + Q_2$$

so that

$$VC = VC_1 + VC_2$$

dividing through by V,

$$C = C_1 + C_2$$

The total capacitance of capacitors in parallel is equal to the sum of the individual capacitors.

EXAMPLE 3.4

Capacitors of 1.5 μF and 2.5 μF respectively are connected in parallel to a p.d. of 120 V, calculate:
(a) *the total charge*
(b) *the charge stored on each capacitor.*

(a) Total capacitance $= C_1 + C_2$

$$= 1.5 \ \mu\text{F} + 2.5 \ \mu\text{F} = \underline{4 \ \mu\text{F}}$$

Total charge $Q = VC$

$$= 120 \times 4 = \underline{480 \ \mu C}$$

(b) Charge on capacitor 1, $Q_1 = VC_1$

$$= 120 \times 1.5 = \underline{180 \ \mu C}$$

Charge on capacitor 2, $Q_2 = VC_2$

$$= 120 \times 2.5 = \underline{300 \ \mu C}$$

3.15 Exercises

1. Draw the lines of force indicating the magnetic fields and their direction for arrangements of magnets shown in Fig. 3.15(a) and (b).

2. By means of a sketch show the telephone-type relay designed to put one circuit *on* and another circuit *off*.

3. Draw a relay circuit which when operated will make for continuous ringing of a bell. Include a reset push.

4. (a) Explain how a magnetic field can produce force on a conductor.

(b) State two ways for increasing this force.

5. Explain what is meant by inductance and how it produces a back e.m.f.

6. Draw an elementary generator with two loops set at right angles.

7. Show the relation between charge, voltage, and capacitance of a capacitor. State the units of each.

8. Describe the parts which constitute a capacitor.

9. If you were given three similar capacitors, show how they could be connected to obtain the maximum charge.

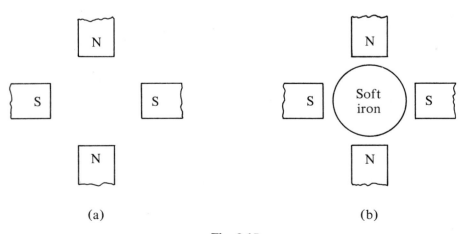

(a)   (b)

Fig. 3.15

10. A formula used in connection with capacitors is

$$\text{Energy in joules} = \tfrac{1}{2}CV^2$$

where C is the capacitance in farads and V the applied voltage.

(a) Find the energy in joules when $C = 540\ \mu F$ and $V = 240\ V$.

(b) Find the voltage when $C = 1700\ \mu F$ and the energy is $102.8\ J$.

4. Measuring instruments and measurements

Electricity meters such as ammeters and voltmeters are known as *indicating instruments*. They indicate the quantity to be measured only while the supply is actually switched on.

The driving force for the movement of a pointer over a scale is based on the effects of an electric current – heating, chemical, or magnetic. Due to its relative simplicity, the principle of action is generally based on the magnetic effect, the instrument being designed to move a pointer needle over a scale proportional to the quantity to be measured.

4.1 Meter reading

With the pointer corresponding to a definite scale line, there should be no difficulty in achieving accuracy providing the reading is taken with the eye directly over the needle and not at an angle. Figure 4.1(a) reads 1 A and Fig. 4.1(b), 35 V. When the reading is not taken directly over the pointer, 'parallax' mistakes occur. These errors are avoided by the insertion of a mirror behind the pointer.

With the needle pointer settling between two scale lines, judgement is required. In Fig. 4.1(c) the reading can be gauged as 67 V. Even greater care is essential when checking the units recorded by the older type of kilowatt-hour (kWh) domestic integrating meter when reading the number of units consumed. It is left as an exercise for the student to check that the diagram in Fig. 4.2 records 2753.54 kWh.

The present trend is to completely simplify scale reading by the installation of electronic *digital* types. Each digit or single number is based on the seven separate parts of the figure:

Individual parts can be separately illuminated by electronic light-emitting diodes (liquid-crystal displays) to make up the digits in the square form of:

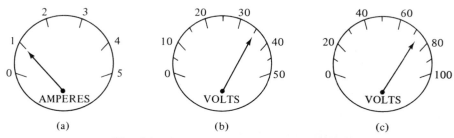

(a)   (b)   (c)

Fig. 4.1   Ammeter and voltmeter readings

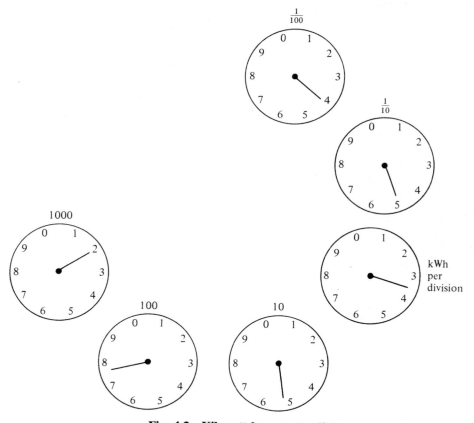

Fig. 4.2   Kilowatt-hour meter dials

4.2 Moving-coil instruments

The modern type of moving-coil meter has many refinements but the basic principle of action is unaltered, being that of a motor with a restricted motion extending over the scale. This instrument has the advantage of giving extreme accuracy, but due to its delicate nature care must be taken when put to actual use.

The main features are shown in Fig. 4.3. Driving torque for force on the moving-coil conductors is provided through the magnetic field from the current led into the coil by phosphor-bronze springs interacting with the magnetic field; the needle being attached to the moving coil. Inside the coil is a soft-iron cylindrical core for the purpose of producing a strong magnetic circuit.

To allow the pointer to rapidly come to its final position, 'damping' is necessary. This is provided by eddy currents generated in the aluminium former. By Lenz's law, the direction of the induced e.m.f. is such as to oppose the motion producing it. Rapid reaching of the quantity to be measured is known as 'dead beat'.

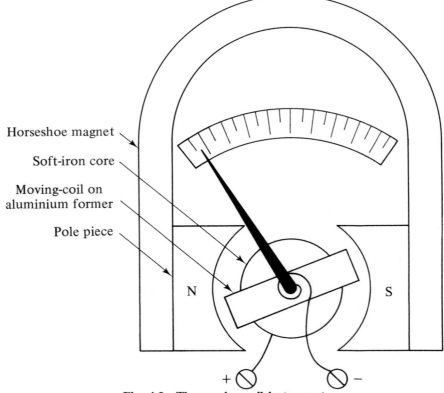

Horseshoe magnet

Soft-iron core

Moving-coil on aluminium former

Pole piece

N

S

+ −

Fig. 4.3 The moving-coil instrument

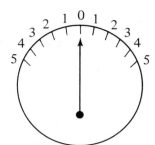

Fig. 4.4 Galvanometer with centre zero

Some form of rectification is necessary for use on a.c. circuits, otherwise the moving-coil meter can only be used for d.c. supplies.

A galvanometer is fitted as part of a potentiometer system. It is usually constructed as a precision moving-coil instrument with a centre zero instead of at the normal left-hand side (Fig. 4.4). The scale is not calibrated in volts or amperes but is simply used for the detection of an e.m.f. and the current direction.

4.3 Moving-iron meters

Generally this instrument has not the accuracy of its moving-coil counter-part. Without careful design the scale would be uneven, being crowded near the zero and more open at the other end (Fig. 4.5). However, the cost is lower, in addition to measuring both a.c. and d.c. with improved sturdiness in construction.

Referring to Fig. 4.5, with current passing through the coil, both of the

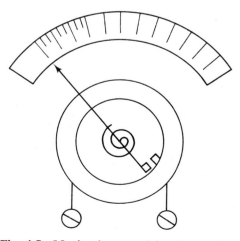

Fig. 4.5 Moving-iron repulsion type meter

internal irons are magnetized to the same magnetic polarity (i.e., two north poles or two south poles) whether the current is direct or alternating, thereby producing repulsion and movement of the needle over the scale. Here the spring is fitted only for control purposes and damping is obtained by a simple air dashpot.

4.4 Instrument connections

Ammeters measure current and are therefore connected in series with the load (Fig. 4.6(a)) otherwise, due to their low resistance, a correspondingly high current will probably result in a severe damage to the instrument.

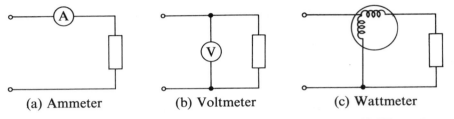

| (a) Ammeter | (b) Voltmeter | (c) Wattmeter |

Fig. 4.6 Instrument connection. (a) Ammeter. (b) Voltmeter. (c) Wattmeter.

Because voltmeters indicate p.d., a parallel connection is required (Fig. 4.6(b)).

As power is obtained by voltage multiplied by current, wattmeters require both voltage and current coils (Fig. 4.6(c)). Single-phase kilowatt-hour (kWh) energy meters are similarly connected.

4.5 Extension of range

The movement of moving-coil instruments – whether voltmeters or ammeters – gives full deflection with a current as low as 75 mA, so that a shunt resistor must be connected in parallel if the instrument is not to be overloaded.

EXAMPLE 4.1

A moving-coil meter has a resistance of 8 Ω and gives a full-scale deflection with a current as low as 10 mA. It is required to read up to (a) 10 A (b) 100 V. Calculate the required resistance in each case.
(a) A shunt resistor is necessary as shown in Fig. 4.7.

$$\text{Current through parallel resistor} = 10 \text{ A} - 10 \text{ mA}$$
$$= (10 - 0.01) \text{ A}$$
$$= 9.99 \text{ A}$$

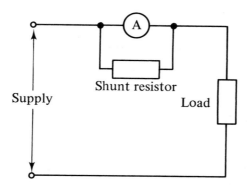

Fig. 4.7   Extension of ammeter range

$$\text{Voltage across meter movement} = IR = 0.01 \times 8$$
$$= 0.08 \text{ V}$$
$$\text{Value of shunt resistor} = \frac{V}{I} = \frac{0.08}{9.99}$$
$$= 0.008 \ \Omega = \underline{8 \text{ m}\Omega}$$

(b) Here a series resistor is essential (Fig. 4.8). As we have seen, the p.d. across the voltmeter movement is 0.08 V.

To read up to 100 V, the voltage across the series resistor

$$= 100 - 0.08 \text{ V}$$
$$= 99.92 \text{ V}$$

$$\text{By Ohm's law, series resistor} = \frac{99.92}{0.01}$$
$$= 9992 \ \Omega = \underline{9.992 \text{ k}\Omega}$$

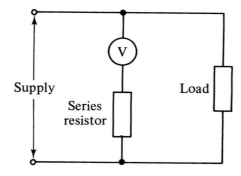

Fig. 4.8   Extension of voltmeter range

$$\text{Alternatively, total resistance} = \frac{100 \text{ V}}{0.01 \text{ A}} = 10\ 000\ \Omega$$

$$\therefore \text{Series-added resistance} = 10\ 000 - 8$$

$$= \underline{9992\ \Omega}$$

4.6 The potentiometer

The use of this arrangement makes for extreme precision as no current is flowing while the reading is taken. Thus no inaccuracies are produced by *IR* voltage drops. Normally the potentiometer is used for the measurement of an e.m.f. although it can be adapted for the determination of resistance or current.

To understand its principle of action, reference is made to Fig. 4.9, where AB is a slide wire of uniform cross-sectional area supplied by one or more cells. One lead of a voltmeter is connected to A and the other end is allowed to make contact along the uniform wire AB. Then as this second lead moves from A to B there will be a corresponding increase in the p.d. as recorded on the voltmeter.

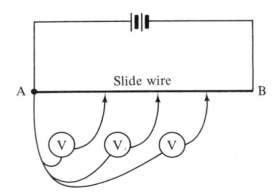

Fig. 4.9   P.D. with contact distance from A

Referring to the circuit of Fig. 4.10, *S* is a standard cell of known e.m.f. and G a galvanometer with a centre zero. By moving the contact along the slide wire, a point will be reached where zero reading will be recorded on the galvanometer. At the same time, the length of A to B (l_1) is noted.

A cell of *x* volts whose e.m.f. is to be measured replaces the standard cell and the contact is moved until again zero reading is recorded on G. This distance is called l_2.

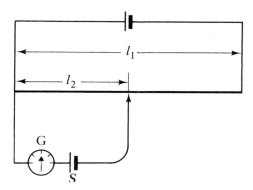

Fig. 4.10   Use of potentiometer for accurate measuring of e.m.f.

Since the ratio of lengths along the slide wire is proportional to the voltages,

$$\frac{l_1}{l_2} = \frac{S}{x}$$

$$x = \frac{l_2}{l_1} \times S \text{ volts}$$

EXAMPLE 4.2

A standard cell of e.m.f. 1.0186 V is balanced against a battery by a potentiometer slide wire. For zero reading on the galvanometer the distance of the contact from the positive end of the slide wire is 250 mm. When the standard cell is replaced by a cell of unknown e.m.f., zero reading is obtained with a contact distance 350 mm. What is the e.m.f. of the unknown cell?

$$\frac{\text{e.m.f. of known cell}}{\text{e.m.f. of unknown cell}} = \frac{\text{contact distance for known cell } (l_1)}{\text{contact distance of unknown cell } (l_2)}$$

$$\text{e.m.f. of unknown cell} = \text{e.m.f. of known cell} \times \frac{l_2}{l_1}$$

$$= \frac{1.0186 \times 350}{250}$$

$$= \underline{1.426 \text{ V}}$$

4.7   Exercises

1. By means of a sketch describe the action of the moving-coil instrument. Why can it only be used on d.c. circuits?

2. Explain the principle of action of the moving-iron meter.

3. Why can moving-iron meters be used on both d.c. and a.c. supplies?

4. What voltage is recorded on the voltmeter shown in Fig. 4.11?

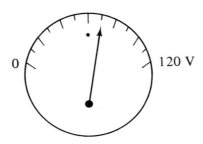

0   120 V

Fig. 4.11

5. A meter gives full-scale deflection with 75 mV. If the resistance of the movement is 5 Ω, what value of further resistance is required to read up to 5 A? Include all circuit connections.

6. An indicating instrument with a resistance of 5 Ω requires 10 mA for full scale deflection. What further resistance is necessary to permit the meter to read up to 25 V? Include all circuit connections.

7. It is required to measure current voltage and power in a circuit. Show by means of a diagram how this can be carried out.

5. Alternating currents

5.1 What is an a.c.?

An alternating current or voltage is a type of supply which is continually changing in direction from positive to negative and then negative to positive.

A primitive form of a.c. may be obtained by connecting a d.c. input to a changeover double pole switch (Fig. 5.1). Operating the switch from position *a* to position *b* produces one cycle of alternating current (Fig. 5.2). The graph depicts the waveform for one complete reversal, producing a flat-topped wave.

5.2 The a.c. loop generator

For standard electrical supplies a.c. generation is obtained by means of rotary motion. Figure 5.3 shows a single turn, or loop of wire, as part of an armature of an a.c. generator, the latter being often termed an *alternator*. The insulated loop is mounted on a shaft and pivoted so as to rotate – either clockwise or anti-clockwise – between magnetic poles, and the ends of the loop are connected to brass slip rings. Pressure is maintained by springs on carbon brushes so that there is continuous contact with the rings thereby enabling leads to be connected to a stationary external circuit.

Figure 5.4 illustrates the slip rings and brushgear of a practical generator.

5.3 Sine wave

We have already seen (Chapter 3) that if a flux consisting of magnetic lines of force is crossed or 'cut' by a wire, e.m.f. is induced in the conductor. Should the wire form part of a complete circuit then current will flow. Referring to Fig. 5.3, the maximum flux is being cut by the sides of the loop on rotation. Therefore at this position the maximum e.m.f. is generated in the circuit. When the coil has rotated 90°, the sides of the turn are momentarily parallel with the field. In this position no flux is cut and therefore no e.m.f. is induced in the armature coil.

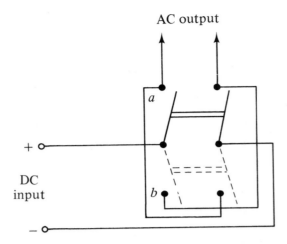

Fig. 5.1   Use of changeover switch for production of a.c.

A further 90° later there is again maximum e.m.f. but now current flows in the reverse direction, and finally reduces to zero at 360° for one complete cycle.

It is important to note that an exactly similar effect is produced where the loop is stationary and the magnetic poles rotate round the armature.

Figure 5.5 depicts the complete waveform for a cycle as traced out by one conductor turn taken at 30° intervals. At these 30° points the upright

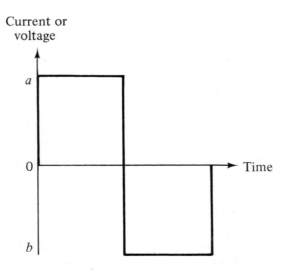

Fig. 5.2   Flat-topped a.c. wave produced by changeover switch

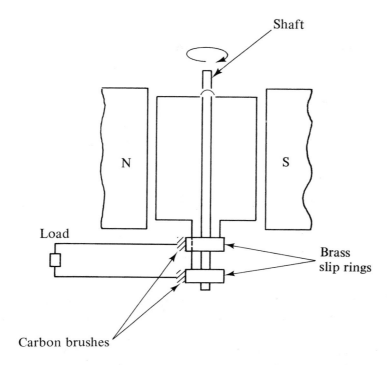

Fig. 5.3 Loop rotation producing an a.c.

lines, called ordinates, represent the instantaneous amount of e.m.f. produced. External connections to a resistor produce a similar shape of waveform for current values.

The positive half-cycle takes place above the degrees baseline, while the negative half-cycle is below. In Great Britain the standard supply is 50 of these cycles per second, so that the time taken to complete 1 cycle is 1/50 (0.02) of a second. Therefore the baseline can be stated in time (parts of a second) instead of degrees.

The unit for cycles per second is the *hertz* (Hz) and this particular wave shape is called the *sine wave*, since in trigonometry, the value of each ordinate is proportional to the sine of the corresponding angle.

5.4 A.C. and D.C. equivalents

Because the current and voltage are continually changing from zero to maximum the problem arises: (a) exactly what value should be taken, and (b) how to make this value equivalent to d.c.?

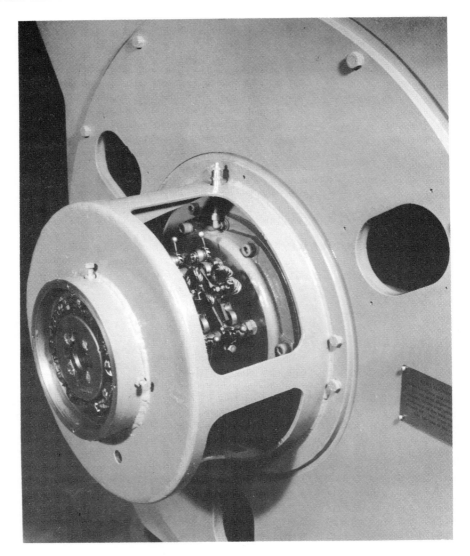

Fig. 5.4 Slip rings and brushgear of an a.c. generator (*Courtesy of GEC Machines Ltd*)

The accepted solution has been found by passing a.c. and d.c., for the same period of time, through similar resistors. The heat rise is measured and if it is the same for both types of supply, then the currents are accepted as being equivalent. In the a.c. case this equivalent value is found to be 0.707 times the maximum amount. As explained in the next section, it is also called the r.m.s. value.

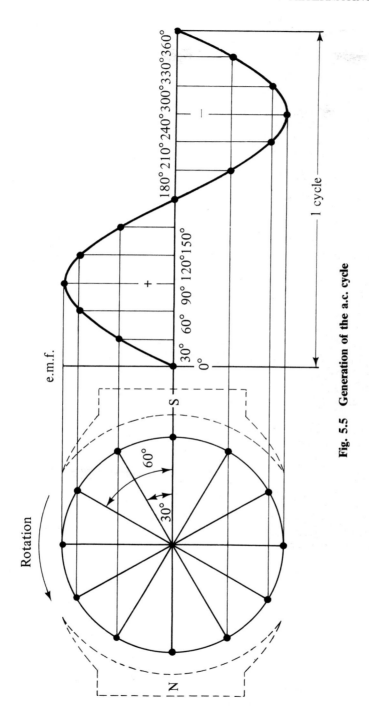

Fig. 5.5 Generation of the a.c. cycle

EXAMPLE 5.1

The standard a.c. voltage is 240 V. What is the maximum voltage?

Unless otherwise stated, a.c. voltages and currents are accepted as being r.m.s. values, thus here the r.m.s. value is 240 V.

$$\text{Now r.m.s.} = 0.7071 \times \text{maximum value}$$

$$\therefore \text{Maximum value} = \frac{\text{r.m.s.}}{0.707}$$

$$= \frac{240}{0.7071} = \underline{339.4 \text{ V}}$$

The example shows that greater care is required when working on alternating current supplies. The peak value of 240 V a.c. may produce a severer shock than 240 V d.c.

5.5   RMS values

The letters RMS stand for 'root mean square', i.e., the square root of the average square, and provide an alternative method for obtaining the equivalent d.c. value.

Each mid-ordinate (Fig. 5.6) which represents e.m.f. or current at a particular instant is squared and the mean (average) value obtained. The square root of this value is the r.m.s. Since both half-waves are similar in shape, only one half or even a quarter need be taken.

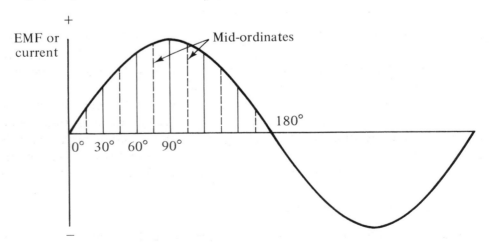

Fig. 5.6   Mid-ordinates for obtaining r.m.s. values

A useful exercise is to trace out the sine wave, then produce the appropriate mid-ordinates and calculate the resultant r.m.s.

5.6 Lagging and leading currents

By the application of current through an inductance coil, a strong magnetic field is built up. Where the supply is a.c. the current is continually changing, bringing a corresponding change in magnetic field. The latter cuts, or passes across, the windings of the inductance coil and induces a voltage in the form of a back e.m.f.

The effect of this induced e.m.f. is to oppose the change in current, resulting in a lagging current, i.e., a current which requires careful study as it lags behind the voltage. Figure 5.7 shows that the current reaches its

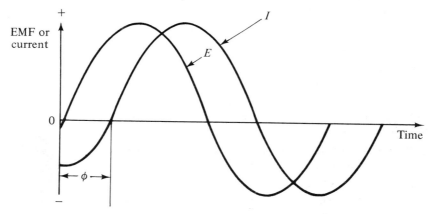

Fig. 5.7 Lagging current

maximum or peak value later in time than the voltage. On a.c. circuits this effect can be very marked as the majority of present-day machinery, such as motors and transformers, consists of coils and is therefore inductive. The symbol ϕ (phi) is the phase angle of lag.

We have seen that a capacitor charge (in coulombs) is proportional to the charging voltage. When a capacitor is connected to a.c. it is continually being charged and discharged, resulting in an alternating current which is proportional to the rate of charge of the voltage, so that when a capacitor forms part of an a.c. circuit it produces a current lead (Fig. 5.8).

5.7 Reactance and impedance

The effect of inductance in opposing the current is called *inductive reactance* (X_L) and is measured in ohms. Impedance (Z) is the combined

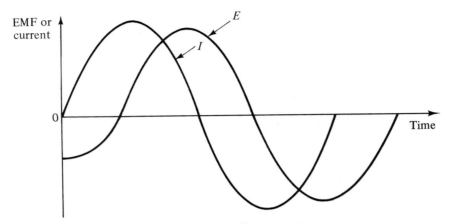

Fig. 5.8 Leading current

effect of both resistance and reactance and may be represented by a
right-angled phasor diagram (Fig. 5.9), which also shows the phase angle ϕ
(phi) of lag. Again capacitors produce capacitive reactance with angle of
lead. Inductive reactance, capacitive reactance, and impedance are known
as *phasor* quantities.

EXAMPLE 5.2

*From the circuit diagram in Fig. 5.10 find (**a**) the impedance (**b**) the value of
resistor R*

(**a**) $$\text{current} = \frac{\text{voltage}}{\text{impedance}}$$

$$\therefore \text{impedance } (Z) = \frac{\text{voltage}}{\text{current}}$$

$$= \frac{200}{4} = \underline{50 \ \Omega}$$

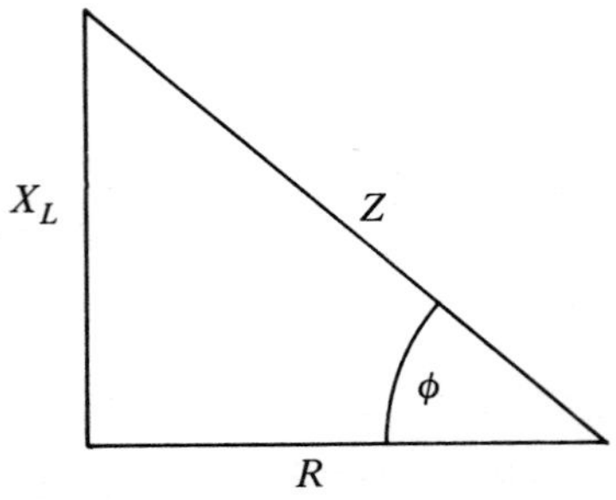

Fig. 5.9 Impedance triangle

64

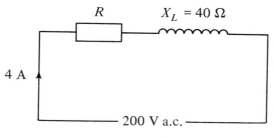

Fig. 5.10

(**b**) Also from the impedance triangle,

$$Z = \sqrt{R^2 + X_L^2}$$

Then squaring both sides,

$$Z^2 = R^2 + X_L^2$$

and transposing,

$$R^2 = Z^2 - X_L^2$$

Finally, taking the square root of both sides,

$$R = \sqrt{Z^2 - X_L^2}$$
$$= \sqrt{50^2 - 40^2}$$
$$= \sqrt{2500 - 1600}$$
$$= \sqrt{900} = \underline{30\ \Omega}$$

5.8 Power factor

Where inductive or capacitive reactance are present in a circuit, the current will respectively lag or lead the voltage. As seen in Figs. 5.7 and 5.8, there is a time or 'phase difference'. Under these circumstances, the product of the voltage and current will not give the power in watts, but must be multiplied by some decimal number – always less than one – called the *power factor*. It is usually stated as a ratio of power in watts to volt-amperes.

However, as an equation power factor may take various forms:

$$\text{Power factor} = \frac{P}{VI}$$

$$= \frac{kV}{kVA}$$

$$= \frac{R}{Z}$$

$$= \cos \phi \qquad \text{where } \phi \text{ is the angle of lag or lead}$$

EXAMPLE 5.3

A single-phase motor delivers 10.44 kW at full load. Instruments registering the electrical input to the motor read as follows:

Voltmeter	*240 V*
Ammeter	*85 A*
Wattmeter	*14 300 W*

Find the efficiency of the motor and the power factor.

$$\text{Percentage efficiency} = \frac{\text{output}}{\text{input}} \times 100$$

$$= \frac{10\,440 \text{ watts}}{14\,300 \text{ watts}} \times 100 = \underline{73\%}$$

$$\text{Power factor} = \frac{P}{VI}$$

$$= \frac{14\,300 \text{ W}}{240 \text{ V} \times 85 \text{ A}} = \underline{0.7 \text{ lagging}}$$

EXAMPLE 5.4

Calculate the current required for a 240 V, 3 kW load when the power factor is (a) 0.9 and (b) 0.6

(a) $P = VI \cos \phi \qquad$ by transposition

$$\therefore I = \frac{P}{V \cos \phi}$$

$$= \frac{3000}{240 \times 0.9} = \underline{13.9 \text{ A}}$$

(b) $I = \dfrac{P}{V \cos \phi}$

$\qquad = \dfrac{3000}{240 \times 0.6} = \underline{20.8 \text{ A}}$

Since low power factor produces a current increase for a given power, the effect is also to raise the power losses (I^2R) for transmission cables in addition to voltage drops. Also, larger sizes of switchgear and cables are necessary to carry the increased currents.

For these reasons, power-factor improvement is encouraged by electricity boards. In the fluorescent fitting, the choke is highly inductive and power-factor improvement is effected by connecting a capacitor across the supply terminals of the fitting.

5.9 Reactive kilovolt-amperes

The power phasor diagram (Fig. 5.11) shows the power (kW) in phase with the current. The reactive kilovolt-amperes (kVAr) is 90° out of phase with the current and it is the result of decreasing the value of kVAr by reducing the phase angle (ϕ) which makes for power improvement.

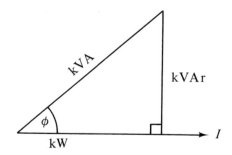

Fig. 5.11 Power phasor diagram

5.10 Transformers

The main purpose of transformers is to change voltage values. In essence the double-wound transformer consits of two windings insulated from each other and linked by a common magnetic field (Fig. 5.12). In the figure, the

Core

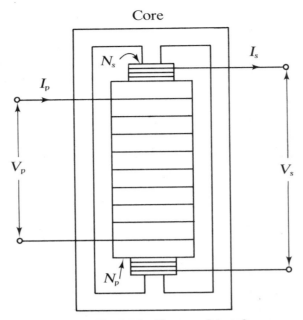

Fig. 5.12 Simple double-wound transformer

following symbols are used:

$$V_p = \text{primary voltage}$$
$$V_s = \text{secondary voltage}$$
$$I_p = \text{primary current}$$
$$I_s = \text{secondary current}$$
$$N_p = \text{primary turns}$$
$$N_s = \text{secondary turns}$$

The core consists of high-permeability steel laminations which may be lightly insulated from each other so as to minimize (a) eddy currents, (b) magnetic flux losses. For safety the lower-voltage winding would be placed nearer to the core.

An a.c. in the primary winding causes an alternating e.m.f. to be induced in the secondary by electromagnetic action. Assuming no losses, the voltage per turn of primary and secondary are equal:

$$\frac{V_p}{N_p} = \frac{V_s}{N_s}$$

and by transposition

$$\frac{V_p}{V_s} = \frac{N_p}{N_s}$$

from which it can be seen that the voltage ratio is equal to the turns ratio. Further, the ampere-turns of the primary and secondary are also equal:

$$I_p N_p = I_s N_s$$

and

$$\frac{I_p}{I_s} = \frac{N_s}{N_p}$$

Hence the current ratio is inversely proportional to the turns ratio.

EXAMPLE 5.5

(a) *Give reasons for laminating the core of a transformer.*
(b) *Draw a connection diagram of a single-phase, double-wound transformer of 240 V primary voltage, showing how the secondary voltages of 4 V, 8 V, and 12 V could be obtained.*
(c) *If the number of turns on the primary of the transformer in (b) is 1920, find the number of turns on the 12 V secondary winding.*

(a) As already stated, a laminated core consisting of thin insulated sheets reduces eddy current. If the core consisted of a solid mass of metal the eddy currents would result in an undue heat rise and damage the insulation of the windings.

(b) The diagram is shown in Fig. 5.13.

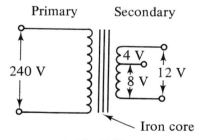

Fig. 5.13

(c)
$$\frac{V_p}{V_s} = \frac{N_p}{N_s}$$

$$\therefore \text{Secondary turns } N_s = \frac{N_p V_s}{V_p}$$

$$= \frac{1920 \times 12}{240} = \underline{96 \text{ turns}}$$

Auto-transformers permit a reduction in cost as, instead of two separate windings, the secondary virtually forms a tapping off the primary (Fig. 5.14). Since the primary and secondary are in physical contact there are severe restrictions to its use. It is not usual to exceed a turns ratio of $2:1$. A particular sphere of application where the restrictions do not apply is for certain motor starters to reduce the heavy starting current. Turns, voltage, and current ratios are calculated as for the double-wound type.

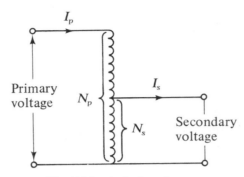

Fig. 5.14   Auto-transformer

5.11   Star and delta

These terms signify two distinct methods of connecting equal (i.e., balanced) loads to a 3-phase supply
(i) *Star* (Fig. 5.15)

$$V_L = \text{line voltage}$$
$$V_P = \text{phase voltage}$$
$$I_L = \text{line current}$$
$$I_P = \text{phase current}$$

Clearly, line current is equal to the phase current but $V_L = \sqrt{3} V_P$
(ii) *Delta* (Fig. 5.16)
  Here

$$V_L = V_P$$

and

$$I_L = \sqrt{3} I_P$$

It will be noted that V_L is the voltage between any two lines. The total 3-phase power in either star or delta is given by

$$P = \sqrt{3} V_L I_L \cos \phi \qquad \text{where } \cos \phi \text{ is the power factor}$$

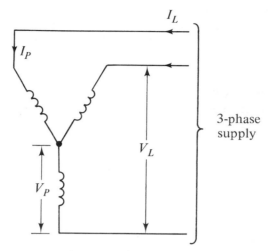

Fig. 5.15   Star connection

or

$$P = 3V_P I_P \cos \phi$$

EXAMPLE 5.6

*A 3-phase load consists of three similar windings, each of impedance 106.6 Ω. The supply between lines is 415 V 50 Hz. Calculate (**a**) the line current (**b**) the total power when the load is (i) star connected (ii) delta connected with a power factor of 0.47.*

(i) *Star connected*

(**a**) Line voltage is equal to $\sqrt{3}$ times the phase voltage,

$$V_L = \sqrt{3}\, V_P$$

$$\therefore V_P = \frac{V_L}{\sqrt{3}} = \frac{415}{\sqrt{3}} = 240 \text{ V}$$

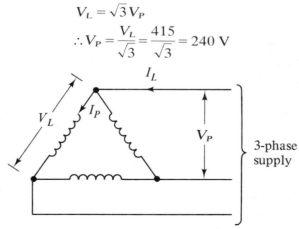

Fig. 5.16   Delta connection

$$\text{Current in each phase} = \frac{\text{phase voltage}}{\text{impedance}}$$

$$= \frac{240}{106.6} = 2.25 \text{ A}$$

Line current = $\underline{2.25 \text{ A}}$

(**b**) Power = $\sqrt{3}\, V_L I_L \cos \phi$

$$= \sqrt{3} \times 415 \times 2.25 \times 0.47 = \underline{762 \text{ W}}$$

Alternatively,

Power = $3 \times$ power in each phase

$$= 3 \times 240 \times 2.25 \times 0.47 = \underline{762 \text{ W}}$$

(ii) *Delta connected*

(**a**) Line and phase voltages are equal.

$$I_P = \frac{\text{phase voltage}}{\text{impedance}}$$

$$= \frac{415}{106.6} = 3.9 \text{ A}$$

$$I_L = \sqrt{3}\, I_P$$

$$= \sqrt{3} \times 3.9 = \underline{6.75 \text{ A}}$$

(**b**) Power = $\sqrt{3}\, V_L I_L \cos \phi$

$$= \sqrt{3} \times 415 \times 6.75 \times 0.47 = \underline{2280 \text{ W}}$$

Alternatively,

Power = $3 \times I_P V_P \cos \phi$

$$= 3 \times 3.9 \times 415 \times 0.47 = \underline{2280 \text{ W}}$$

5.12 Exercises

1. (a) A 240 V/110 V single-phase, double-wound step-down transformer has a primary winding of 960 turns and a full-load secondary current of 5 A. Ignoring losses, calculate:
   (i) the number of turns in the secondary winding
   (ii) the full-load primary current.
   (b) Draw and label a circuit diagram of a bell transformer.
2. A 250 V single-phase motor has an output of 1500 W. If the full-load efficiency of the motor is 75 per cent and its power factor is 0.8, calculate:
   (a) the input power in watts
   (b) the current taken from the supply.

3. The following formula is used in a.c. calculations: $Z = \sqrt{R^2 + X^2}$, where Z is the impedance, R is resistance, and X is reactance, all in ohms. Find the value of X, when $Z = 6.8$ and $R = 4.5\,\Omega$.

4. (a) Explain the meaning of 'power factor'.

    (b) A 240 V single phase motor gives its full-load output of 10 kW with an efficiency of 85 per cent and at a power factor of 0.7 lagging. Calculate the current input to the motor and put all values in a circuit diagram.

5. (a) State the relationships between kW, kVa, and power factor.

    (b) A 240 V single-phase motor is working on load with an efficiency of 85 per cent and at a power factor of 0.75 lagging. If the current from the supply is 24 A, find the motor output in kW.

6. Three resistors, each of 20 Ω, are connected to a 3-phase supply. If the line voltage is 415 V, calculate the line current and total power in (a) star and (b) delta connections.

Multiple choice

7. An a.c. is a type of supply which is:
(a) continually changing in value
(b) continually reversing in polarity
(c) opposite to d.c.
(d) an oscillating current

8. Frequency is:
(a) the number of sine waves
(b) speed of the a.c.
(c) number of cycles per second
(d) number of electrons/second

9. The time for 1 cycle is on 100 Hz supply is:
(a) 0.05 sec
(b) 0.50 sec
(c) 0.01 sec
(d) 0.02 sec

10. RMS value is:
(a) the average value
(b) the square root of the average value
(c) the square root of the average square
(d) the square root value

11. A lagging current is caused by:
(a) a phase difference
(b) an inductor
(c) time difference
(d) flux cut

5.13 Crossword puzzle

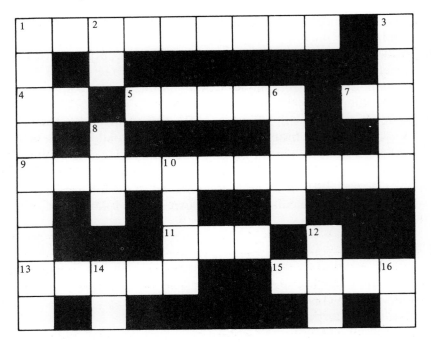

Fig. 5.17

CLUES

ACROSS

1 Continuous action of an a.c.
4 Alternating current
5 Cycles per second
7 Power
9 Will operate only on a.c.
11 Part of a north pole
13 Complete a.c. wave
15 EMF set up by current changes

DOWN

1 Inductive and capacitive
2 Apparent power
3 Energy per unit time
6 Value of an a.c. twice per cycle
8 Micro—, a.c. switch
10 Standard a.c. wave
12 Ohm's
14 Alternative abbreviation to d.c.
16 10^3 amperes

6. Secondary cells

6.1 Primary cells

For the reason that they are in common use for bells, torches and certain types of equipment – usually electronic – a brief description of primary cells is merited. Almost any two different metals when adjacent to each other and separated by a liquid, called the *electrolyte*, will set up an e.m.f. The discovery of this source of electrical energy is credited to an Italian scientist named Galvani. It is enlightening to briefly trace the development from the basic form. About 1770 Galvani had a frog's leg hung by a copper hook and noticed a twitching whenever the leg touched an iron balcony.

Further experiments led to the simple primary cell consisting of copper – later replaced by carbon – and zinc immersed in dilute sulphuric acid (Fig. 6.1(a)). With the plates connected to an external circuit, current flows from the positive to a load and back to the negative terminal. However, the current soon decreases owing to hydrogen bubbles forming on the copper plate and constituting a high-resistance path.

Figure 6.1(b) depicts a more modern type of Leclanché type cell. For portability the electrolyte is made into a paste. One salient feature is the manganese dioxide depolarizer, which tends to neutralize the hydrogen bubbles, thus allowing the cell to deliver current for longer periods. The e.m.f. is about 1.5 V. Due to the drive to compactness and longer life, developments have led to the use of many other materials placed in a stack formation.

6.2 Secondary-cell essentials

If two lead plates are immersed in dilute sulphuric acid and connected to a d.c. supply, certain chemical changes take place in the lead plates. The plate connected to the positive connection turns brown and the other slate grey.

With the d.c. supply disconnected, the cell itself now has the property of delivering current with a voltage of about 2 V. This process is reversible and is in sharp contrast to the primary cell where once the chemicals have been used up, it will no longer give out current. Cells may be connected in series or parallel to form a battery.

In modern secondary cells, because the life largely depends upon the design of the positive plate, it is formed into a fine network for the

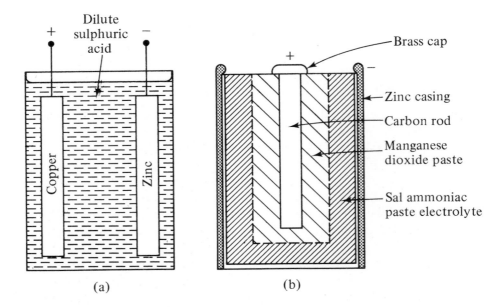

Fig. 6.1 Primary cells

purpose of increasing the surface area. The negative plate of lead alloy is constructed into open grids filled with lead oxide paste (Fig. 6.2(a) and (b)).

Insulated separators between positive and negative plates make for compactness. The additional negative plate is for the purpose of minimizing the tendency to buckle of the positive plate (Fig. 6.3).

Both primary and secondary cells are examples of the chemical effect of an electric current. Often termed *accumulators*, secondary cells are of great practical importance in providing vital emergency supplies and for certain industrial processes. In case of shutdowns in power stations they are relied upon to carry the load, and they are also of importance, in this modern age, to ensure continuous computer supplies. In certain public buildings such as cinemas and theatres, a secondary emergency supply is a compulsory legal requirement.

The capacity of a cell is stated in ampere-hours (Ah), being the delivery current in amperes multiplied by output time in hours, so that a battery with a capacity of 80 Ah at a 10 h rate would permit an 8 A discharge for 10 hours, but not for a high rate of 16 A for 5 hours as this could damage the cell.

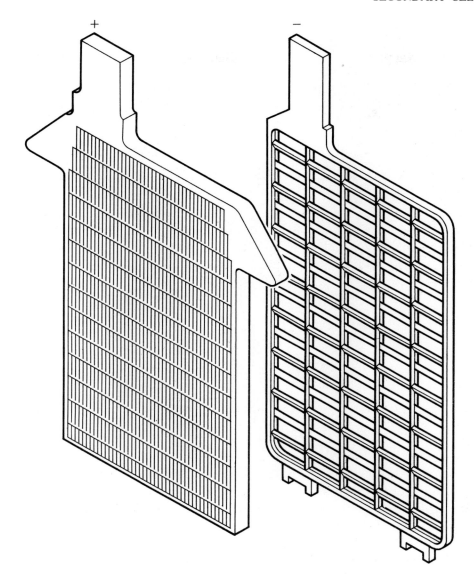

Fig. 6.2(a) Modern secondary cell with grid-type plates

EXAMPLE 6.1

A secondary cell is charged at 30 A for 10 h, calculate (**a**) *the cell capacity and* (**b**) *the current which could flow for a discharge of 15 h.*

(**a**) Cell capacity $= 30 \times 10 = \underline{300 \text{ Ah}}$

(**b**) Discharge current $= \dfrac{300}{15} = \underline{20 \text{ A}}$

Fig. 6.2(b) Modern secondary cell with grid-type plates (*Courtesy of Chloride Alcad Ltd*)

(It should be observed that the cell capacity also denotes the quantity of electricity.)

6.3 Charging

The state of charge can be checked by a hydrometer (Fig. 6.4) showing the *specific gravity* (S.G.) of the electrolyte. Here the specific gravity means

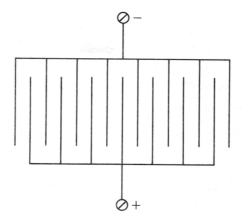

Fig. 6.3   Plate arrangement

the weight of a volume of the electrolyte compared to the weight of an equal volume of water. The nozzle is dipped into the electrolyte, and a small sample obtained by squeezing and then releasing the top rubber bulb. The S.G. of a cell will probably vary between 1.280 when fully charged and 1.150 on discharge (these values are pronounced as 'twelve eighty' and 'eleven fifty' respectively). For exact values, manufacturers' instruction sheets should be consulted.

The output voltage when the cell is fully charged varies from 2.1 to 2.6 V. On discharge it must not be allowed to fall below 1.86 V. For higher voltages, cells are connected in series, while parallel connection produces increased capacity.

The basic charging circuit consists of an external d.c. supply of a higher voltage than 2.7 V per cell. It is connected with the positive of the external circuit to the secondary cell positive connection, and the negative in a similar manner (Fig. 6.5).

Gassing from the cells will start when the voltage per cell is in the region of 2.3–2.6 V. Charging is completed when the voltage remains stationary for about one to three hours depending on the type.

Methods of charging vary. Certain manufacturers advocate *trickle charging* by a low charging current which maintains the cell voltages and specific gravity at their correct values. In this manner the battery is ready for use. On discharge both plates tend to change to lead sulphate. Alternative charging is by *constant current*; with the circuit as shown in Fig. 6.5, as the battery voltage rises during charge, the series resistor is reduced in order to increase the charging voltage. For charges working from a.c. mains, a tapped secondary is often provided on the transformer.

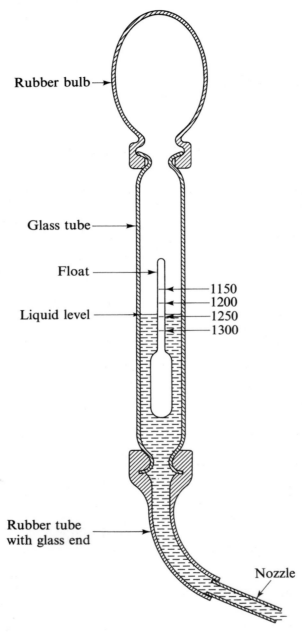

Fig. 6.4   Hydrometer

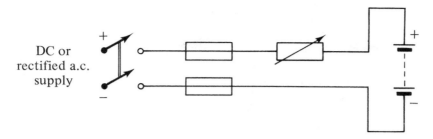

Fig. 6.5   Basic charging circuit

Control may be either manual or automatic. For *constant voltage* charging, the charging supply is connected in parallel with the battery and load. A voltage of 2.3–2.4 V per cell is applied directly to the battery at the beginning and a heavy current flows. With an increasing battery e.m.f. the current will fall. A circuit resistance prevents too heavy a current at commencement.

6.4   Maintenance

To maintain cells in good condition observe the following:

1. Bolted connections must be tight and smeared with petroleum jelly.
2. Cells should be kept in dry, cool premises and must be accessible for testing and topping up. The room should be well ventilated, light, and clean.
3. Basic electrolyte should consist of sulphuric acid to BS 3031.
4. To allow for evaporation pour distilled water into sulphuric acid and not sulphuric acid into distilled water.
5. Cells should not be allowed to stand in an uncharged state.
6. To avoid cell short-circuits, clear away any sediment which may fall to the bottom of the container.
7. Keep cells away from naked flames at all times.
8. Level of electrolyte should always be above the plates.

6.5   Tubular cells

These are a development on flat lead plates. They have an increased capacity up to 2000 Ah and are specially designed to withstand frequent charging and discharging. They deliver high power at low and medium rates of discharge and have the advantage of working well under tough conditions.

In this type of cell, positive plates consist of lead alloy spines filled with a mixture of lead oxide. The tubes are designed to maintain the active material in contact with conducting spines during the period of expansion and contraction which occurs during charge and discharge. This enables them to be more resistant to the strains which might break up other types of plates.

Some uses are for modern cargo and passenger ships as well as to provide emergency lighting, fire-existinguishing sprinkler services, standby and other services.

6.6 Nickel-cadmium cell

Under the heading of alkaline cell there are two types – nickel-iron and nickel-cadmium. The latter is normally fitted and forms a distinct rival to the older lead-acid secondary, in spite of the fact that the efficiency and terminal voltage (1.2 V/cell) are lower and the initial cost is higher.

As against these disadvantages, they have a long life up to 25 years, are extremely robust, and show little changes in specific gravity for long periods and so require little topping up.

In the nickel-cadmium cell (Fig. 6.6) the positive and negative plates are of similar construction. They consist of pockets made from finely perforated steel strips. A form of nickel is used for the positive plate and the metal cadmium for the negative. The electrolyte solution is mainly of a pure potassium hydroxide liquid. Plates are housed in steel or plastic containers.

6.7 Corrosion and plating

Corrosion is an electrolytic action and in some ways resembles that of a primary cell so that there is an actual migration of atomic particles called ions, or an eating away of the metals. In damp situations special care is required when fitting steel conduit trunking or copper sheath of mineral insulated cable which is liable to come in contact with dissimilar metals. On the other hand, this action is usefully employed for the process of chromium and other forms of electroplating.

6.8 Calculations

Calculations are mainly based on Ohm's law as applied to secondary cells. Electromotive force (E) is defined as the open-circuit voltage or voltage

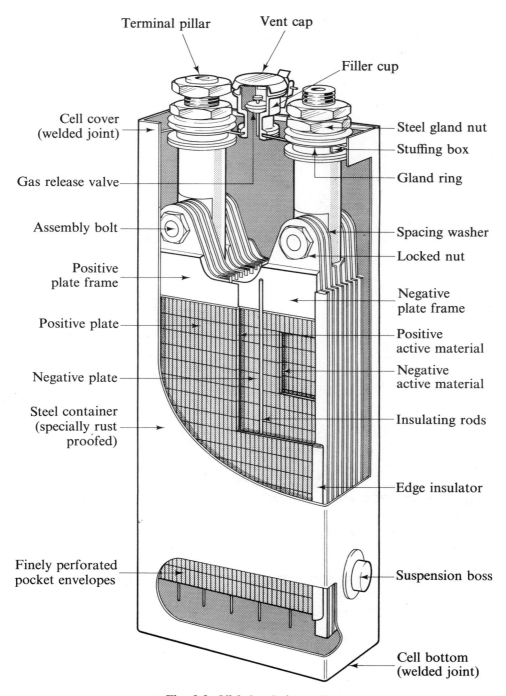

Fig. 6.6 Nickel-cadmium cell

between the positive and negative terminals when there is no current output (I). With current flowing there is a drop in the cell voltage due to the internal cell resistance (r), leading to the equation

$$V = E - Ir$$

V = terminal voltage when delivering current

or

$$E = V + Ir$$

r = internal cell resistance due to the plate and electrolyte materials

Ir = internal voltage drop

EXAMPLE 6.2

A cell with an e.m.f. of 2.3 V has an internal resistance of 0.03 Ω. Calculate the terminal voltage with a current of 10 A flowing.

$$V = E - Ir$$

$$= 2.3 - 10 \times 0.03$$

$$= 2.3 - 0.3 = \underline{2 \text{ V}}$$

EXAMPLE 6.3

If the open-circuit voltage of a secondary cell is 2.2 V and the voltage drops to 2.05 V due to a load current of 5 A, what is the cell resistance?

$$E = V + Ir$$

$$Ir = E - V$$

$$r = \frac{E - V}{I}$$

$$= \frac{2.2 - 2.05}{5} = \underline{0.03 \text{ Ω}}$$

EXAMPLE 6.4

Ten cells, each of e.m.f. 2.1 V and internal resistance 0.05 Ω, are connected in series. Determine the output voltage with a current of 5 A.

84

$$\text{Total e.m.f.} = 10 \times 2.1$$
$$= 21 \text{ V}$$

Total internal voltage drop
$$= 10 \times 5 \times 0.05$$
$$= 2.5 \text{ V}$$

$$\text{Output terminal voltage} = 21 - 2.5 = \underline{18.5 \text{ V}}$$

EXAMPLE 6.5

A secondary cell with an Ah efficiency of 85 per cent is discharging for a period of 10 hours. Assuming the discharging current is 5 A flowing continually for 5 hours, calculate the average charging current.

$$\text{Efficiency} = \frac{\text{output}}{\text{input}} = \frac{\text{Ah on discharge}}{\text{Ah on charge}}$$

$$\therefore \frac{85}{100} = \frac{10 \times 5}{I \times 5} \qquad \text{where } I = \text{charging current}$$

$$\therefore I = \frac{10 \times 5 \times 100}{85 \times 5} = \underline{11.8 \text{ A}}$$

EXAMPLE 6.6

Six cells each with an e.m.f. of 2.1 V and internal resistance of 0.4 Ω are connected in parallel to a load of resistance 0.5 Ω. Calculate the load current.

$$\text{Total e.m.f. of 6 cells in parallel} = 2.1 \text{ V}$$

$$\text{Total internal resistance} = \frac{0.4}{6} = 0.066 \text{ Ω}$$

$$\text{current} = \frac{\text{total e.m.f.}}{\text{total resistance}}$$

$$= \frac{2.1}{0.066 + 0.5} = \underline{3.7 \text{ A}}$$

6.9 Exercises

1. Describe the essential differences between primary and secondary cells. Give examples of the use of each type.

2. Explain certain of the changes which occur in a lead-acid cell during charge and discharge.

3. Describe the lead-acid and nickel-cadmium secondary cells.

4. A battery with an e.m.f. of 15 V and total internal resistance of 0.15 Ω is connected to a load of resistance 2.35 Ω. Determine:

(a) the current flowing

(b) the voltage at the battery terminals on load.

5. A voltmeter connected across a battery indicates 12 V when no current is supplied. When a current of 8 A is taken from the battery the voltmeter indicates 11.5 V. Explain why this happens. What will be the reading of the voltmeter when the battery supplies a current of 16 A?

6. A cell with an e.m.f. of 2.3 V has an internal resistance of 0.03 Ω. Calculate the terminal voltage with a current of 10 A flowing.

7. If the open-circuit voltage of a secondary is 2.2 V and drops to 2.05 V under a load of 5 A, what is the internal resistance?

8. A battery is charged at 10 A for a period of $5\frac{1}{2}$ h. If it gives an output of 7.5 A for 6 h, calculate the ampere-hour efficiency.

9. Describe various charging methods for secondary cells. On discharge what should be the lowest voltage?

7. Electrical heating

Heating is probably one of the most basic forms of electricity. Whenever current flows through a conductor, due to its resistance there is an inevitable tendency to a heat rise, which grows as the current increases. For this reason, one of the objects of correct cable selection is to select a large enough size in order to reduce this heat rise to a minimum value. Otherwise there is the possibility of damage to the cable insulation.

On the other hand, electric heaters, cookers, and allied appliances are specifically designed to produce the maximum heat increase with the minimum current. The ordinary electric lamp is another example; here the tungsten filament is made to glow white-hot to give out light.

7.1 Temperature and heat

These terms must not be confused as they have distinct meanings. Temperature simply indicates the *level* of heat, i.e., how hot is a substance or medium such as air. It is normally measured by a thermometer in degrees Celcius (often called Centigrade) and shortened to °C, which is pronounced as 'degrees C'.

A few typical values gives some indication of the wide band of temperature change:

	°C
Tungsten lamp filament when alight	2–3000
Steel when heated to a bright cherry-red	900
Current ratings of PVC insulated cables, as given in the IEE tables, are based on a working temperature of	30
Comfortable room temperature	16–18

In physics and general scientific work, degrees Kelvin (K) are employed instead of °C. This Celcius scale has replaced Fahrenheit temperature (°F). However, as this latter scale is often seen on thermometers, the relation between the two systems of temperature measurement should be noted (Fig. 7.1).

Since 180 °F (212−32) is equal to 100 °C, it can be seen that

$$°F = \frac{9}{5}°C + 32$$

By transposition, $°C = (°F - 32)\frac{5}{9}$

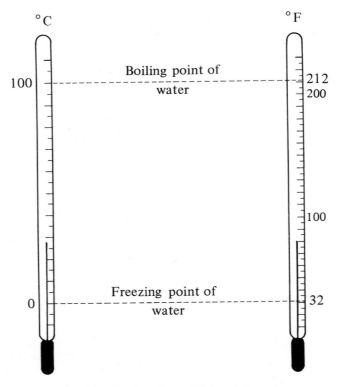

Fig. 7.1   Centigrade and Fahrenheit scales

EXAMPLE 7.1

Convert (**a**) 30 °C *to* °F (**b**) 140 °F *to* °C.

(**a**) $\dfrac{9}{5} \times 30 + 32 = \underline{86\ °F}$

(**b**) $(140 - 32)\dfrac{5}{9} = \underline{60\ °C}$

7.2   Heat

The term must be clearly understood as relating to a form of energy. *Joules* is the basic unit and is the same as that used for electrical energy, and serves to illustrate that electrical energy is easily converted into heat energy.

88

Specific heat capacity is defined as the amount of heat (in joules) required to raise the temperature of 1 kg of a substance by 1 °C. This leads to the fundamental heat equation:

Heat energy (J) = mass of material (kg) × specific heat capacity
(J/kg °C) × temperature change (°C)

or in algebraic terms,

$$W = mc\theta \ \text{joules}$$

Some representative specific heat capacities in J/kg °C:

Brass	390
Steel	511
Air	1010
Oil	2000
Water	4200

EXAMPLE 7.2

A specimen of iron has a specific heat capacity of 500 J/kg °C. If the iron has a mass of 200 kg, calculate (a) the heat required to raise the temperature of iron by 20 °C (b) the power necessary if the heat rise is to take place in five minutes.

(a) $W = mc\theta$
$200 \times 500 \times 20 \ \text{joules} = \underline{2 \ \text{MJ}}$

(b) Also,
$W = Pt$ where P is power in watts
                     t is time in seconds

$$\therefore P = \frac{W}{t}$$

$$= \frac{2 \times 10^6}{5 \times 60} = \underline{6.67 \ \text{kW}}$$

(N.B. The number 60 in the denominator is inserted to convert minutes into seconds.)

EXAMPLE 7.3

A tank contains 1300 kg of oil at an initial temperature of 15 °C. If the temperature of the oil is to rise to 55 °C in 2 hours, determine the heat energy to effect this increase in temperature. Take specific heat capacity of oil as

$2000\ J/kg\ °C.$

$$W = mc\theta$$
$$= 1300 \times (55 - 15) \times 2000$$
$$= 1300 \times 40 \times 2000$$
$$= 104\ 000\ 000\ J$$
$$= \frac{104\ 000\ 000}{3\ 600\ 000}\ kWh = \underline{29\ kWh}$$

(N.B. 3 600 000 joules equal 1 kWh.)

EXAMPLE 7.4

A water heater holding 48 litres of water is heated by means of an immersion heater. Determine the time necessary to raise the temperature of water from 15 °C to 70 °C assuming a power input of 4 kW when:
(**a**) *there is no loss of heat*
(**b**) *the efficiency of the operation is 80 per cent.*
(1 *litre of water has a mass of 1 kg. Specific heat capacity of water is* 4.2 *kJ/kg °C*.)

(**a**) $W = mc\theta$
$$= 48 \times 4.2 \times (70 - 15)$$
$$= 48 \times 4.2 \times 55$$
$$= 11\ 088\ kJ$$

Also, Energy = power × time

$$\therefore t = \frac{W\ (kJ)}{P\ (kW)}$$
$$= \frac{11\ 088}{4}\ \text{seconds} = \underline{46\ min,\ 12\ sec}$$

(**b**) Efficiency $= \dfrac{\text{output}}{\text{input}}$

$$\therefore \frac{80}{100} = \frac{11\ 088\ kJ}{\text{input}}$$
$$\text{input} = \frac{11\ 088 \times 100}{80}$$
$$= 13\ 860\ kJ$$
$$t = \frac{W}{P}$$
$$= \frac{13\ 860}{4} = \underline{57\ min,\ 45\ sec}$$

7.3 Thermostats

Electric space- and water-heating temperatures may be automatically controlled by thermostats. Figure 7.2 illustrates the basic principle of operation for room heating. The moving section responsible for the make-and-break action consists of two metals in firm contact and with different rates of expansion. As the temperature changes, the metals expand or contract at different rates, causing the bimetal leaf to bend. At predetermined temperatures, usually effected by a setting on a dial, curving of the bimetal leaf makes contact which enables the heater to come into action. Contact is broken as the temperature drops from this set figure and remakes with temperature rise.

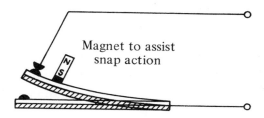

Magnet to assist
snap action

Fig. 7.2   Bimetal action of thermostat

To effect a positive snap action and so minimize arcing, the magnet makes for rapid make and break. This is often assisted by a small accelerator heater in the form of a resistance wire.

Positioning of the thermostat for space heating plays an important part. It should be fixed in a position which is free from draughts, heat radiation, or rays of the sun.

Immersion-heater thermostats are usually of the stem type. They may be constructed from aluminium, brass, or nickel iron so that the resulting differential expansion operates a micro-gap switch, members being enclosed in a dust-excluding moulded plastic cover. Different stem lengths provide for variations in range of temperatures.

7.4   The simmerstat

Three-heat switches which enable elements to be connected in series, singly, or in parallel (Fig. 7.3), although no longer fitted for the heat control of electric cookers, are still used to obtain heat variations for certain appliances. Different heats from fan heaters are often effected by the 3-heat switch.

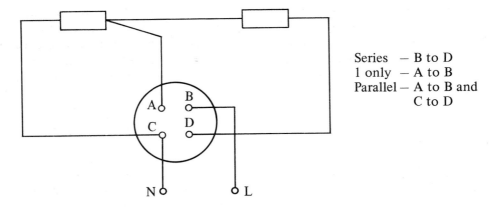

Series   — B to D
1 only   — A to B
Parallel — A to B and
               C to D

Fig. 7.3   Series-parallel switch

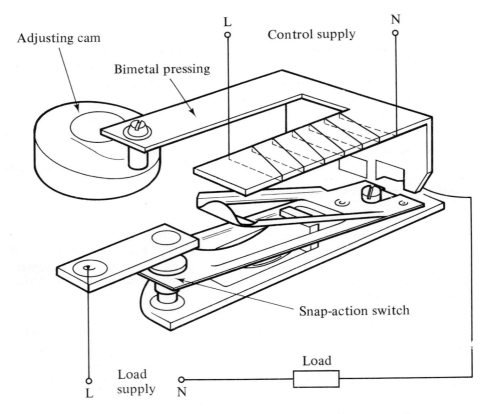

Fig. 7.4   The Simmerstat (*Courtesy of Satchwell Sunvic Ltd*)

Present-day cookers employ simmerstats (Fig. 7.4). They give a much finer control for both plate and oven elements. The operation principle depends upon the opening and closing of a snap-action switch at precise time intervals. Variable control is obtained by a switch knob which turns the adjusting cam and in this way alters the switch on-and-off time intervals.

7.5 Heat sinks

The name is partly self-explanatory. They are used to prevent heat rise in semiconductors and other sensitive (usually electronic) devices. Fitting a heat sink diverts heat away from the electrical component which, in one form, is clamped on to a metal piece. Improvement is effected by correct siting so that air is allowed to pass along the arrangement.

7.6 Exercises

1. State the advantages and disadvantages of heating by electricity.

2. Draw a metal clamp which could be effective to serve as a heat sink.

3. (a) What is the difference between temperature and heat?
   (b) Convert 75 °C to °F and 75 °F to °C.

4. A heating element is rated at 1500 W, 240 V. Calculate:
   (a) the current taken
   (b) the working resistance
   (c) the heat in joules produced by the element during a continuous period of 2 hours.

5. Describe the action of a thermostat for
   (a) space-heating control
   (b) an immersion heater.

6. Calculate the time taken by a 3 kW electric kettle to raise the temperature of 1.5 litres of water from 15 °C to boiling point. Assume the efficiency of the kettle to be 90 per cent. Specific heat capacity of water = 4.2 kJ/kg °C. (1 litre of water has a mass of 1 kg.)

8. Mechanics

Here we shall deal with some simple machines, or parts of a machine, which have the object of making for ease in lifting loads.

The operation of lifting is by no means a new problem. Primitive man probably worked on small tree-trunks as a lever for digging up boulders to make caves, or for their removal when blocking paths. The upward movement of gigantic stones forming the Stonehenge lintels (in Wiltshire) was probably carried out by utilizing the inclined-plane principle (see Sec. 8.5), and also applied to moving the enormous blocks required for building the Egyptian pyramids.

The utilization of modern mechanical-engineering principles enables the maximum output to be obtained from machines with the minimum effort. They also supply means for sound planning and for the derivation of exact calculations.

8.1 Mass and force

Mass may be understood as the amount of material in a metal or plastic material (usually referred to as a body) and is measured in kilograms (kg).

Force is defined as that which, when acting on a mass, moves or tends to move the body forming the mass. It is measured in newtons (N).

Gravity exerts a downward force of 9.81 N on a mass of 1 kg. By converting mass (in kg) to weight (in newtons), the constant of 9.81 acting as a multiplier must be applied.

8.2 Mechanical work (*W*)

Energy is the ability to do work, so that both concepts are measured in joules (J). The work done in joules is equal to the force (N) multiplied by the distance (m) moved of an object.

EXAMPLE 8.1

A 3-phase motor is hauled along a floor a distance of 9.75 m by a force of 25 N. What is the work done?

$$\text{Work done} = \text{force} \times \text{distance}$$
$$= 25 \times 9.75$$
$$= \underline{243.75 \text{ J}}$$

94

EXAMPLE 8.2

In order to raise a transformer to a height of 5 m, the work done is 5000 J. Calculate the force required.

$$W = Fd$$

$$\therefore F = \frac{W}{d}$$

$$= \frac{5000}{5} = \underline{1000 \text{ N}}$$

8.3 Moments of a force

Moments are often referred to as turning moments because they represent the turning effect of a force. With a force of F newtons applied at a distance d metres from the pivot at O (Fig. 8.1), then the moment of the force about O is given by Fd newton metres (Nm).

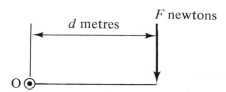

Fig. 8.1   Torque or moment of a force at pivot O = Fd newton-metres

EXAMPLE 8.3

A force of 200 N is applied to the end of a spanner at a distance of 250 mm from the nut centre (Fig. 8.2), what is the turning moment?

$$\text{Turning moment} = Fd \text{ joules}$$

$$= 200 \times 250 \times 10^{-3} = \underline{50 \text{ Nm}}$$

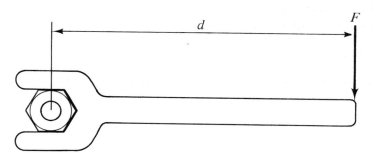

Fig. 8.2   Turning moment of a spanner

8.4 Levers

The actions of levers and their calculations are based on the principle of moments. By use of a lever, a large load can be raised by a small effort. The same principle is effectively applied to crowbars, clawhammers, and many parts of machines.

Referring to Fig. 8.3, the downward force F_1 multiplied by the distance d_1 from the pivot or fulcrum is equal to the upward force F_2 multiplied by d_2.

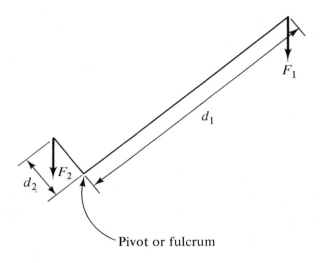

Fig. 8.3 Diagram for level calculations

EXAMPLE 8.4

A load of 27 kg is placed 200 mm from the fulcrum of a lever. What force must be exerted at a distance of 1 m from the other side of the fulcrum in order to raise the load?

From the principle of moments,

$$F_1 d_2 = F_2 d_2$$

$$\text{Required force } F_1 = \frac{27 \times 9.81 \times 200}{1000} \quad \text{(N.B. } d_1 = 1 \text{ m)}$$

$$= \underline{53 \text{ N}}$$

8.5 Inclined plane

Here a smooth flat sloping surface is adopted for raising loads. Work done along the slope equals work done vertically upwards, so that from Fig. 8.4,

$$F_1 d_1 = F_2 d_2$$

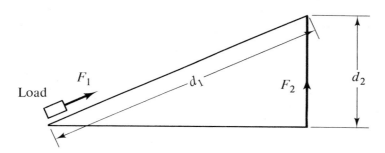

Fig. 8.4 Inclined plane

EXAMPLE 8.5

An inclined plane is employed to raise a generator to a height of 20 m from its initial position. Calculate the force required to raise the generator if the slope distance is 140 m. Neglect losses due to surface friction.

$$\text{Weight of } 400 \text{ kg} = 400 \times 9.81$$
$$= 3924 \text{ N}$$

Now, work done by effort = work done on load

$$F \times 140 = 3924 \times 20$$
$$\therefore F = \frac{3924 \times 20}{140} = \underline{560.6 \text{ N}}$$

8.6 Screw jack

The common straight-sided screw or bolt is a form of inclined plane since the threads are set at an angle. A simple form is shown in Fig. 8.5 (for raising heavier weights the pointed threads would be replaced by collar type with straight sides).

By turning the arm in an anti-clockwise direction through one revolution, the load is raised to a height of one screw pitch. It should be noted that a screw pitch (p) is the distance between two threads.

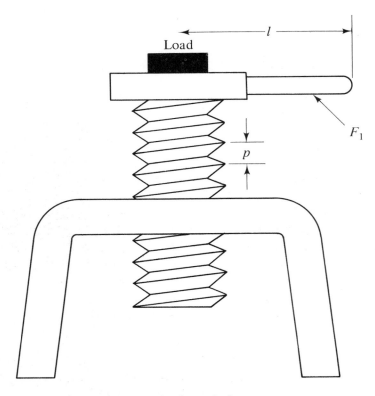

Fig. 8.5   Screw jack

Here again, if losses are not taken into account the work done by the effort and the work done on load are equal.

Assuming a force of F_1 is exerted at the end of the arm of length l and since the distance moved through one revolution is equal to $2\pi l$,

$$F_1 \times 2\pi l = \text{weight of load} \times \text{pitch distance}$$

EXAMPLE 8.6

A load of 150 kg is placed on the head of a screw jack. If the screw pitch is 8 mm and the arm length is 100 mm, determine the force required to lift the load when the efficiency of the operation is 60 per cent.

$$\text{Efficiency} = \frac{\text{output}}{\text{input}}$$

$$= \frac{\text{work done on load}}{\text{work done on effort}}$$

$$\frac{60}{100} = \frac{\text{load force} \times \text{pitch distance}}{\text{effort} \times 2\pi l}$$

$$\frac{60}{100} = \frac{150 \times 9.81 \times 8 \times 10^{-3}}{F \times 2\pi \times 100 \times 10^{-3}}$$

$$F = \frac{150 \times 9.81 \times 8 \times 10^{-3} \times 100}{2\pi \times 100 \times 10^{-3} \times 60} = \underline{31.2\ \text{N}}$$

8.7 Pulley systems

A pull applied at E (Fig. 8.6) serves as a convenient method for lifting certain loads otherwise there is no gain as, disregarding losses, the pulling force and the load weight are equal. To reduce the force necessary to raise a given load, the arrangement must be made up of more pulley wheels.

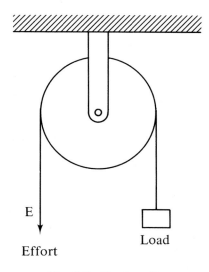

E

Effort

Load

Fig. 8.6 Single pulley

An examination of the two-pulley system (Fig. 8.7) will show that, when in operation, the distance moved by effort will be double that of the load, resulting in a halving of the load force.

This principle enables the use of more pulleys to bring yet a further effort decrease. However, the resistance offered by the arrangement limits the number of pulleys which could be usefully employed.

99

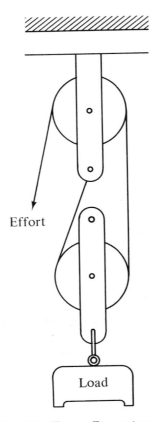

Fig. 8.7 Two-pulley system

EXAMPLE 8.7

Assuming four pulley wheels are fitted to raise a load of 300 kg to a height of 3 m from its original position, calculate the effort required.

Work done by effort = work done on load
With a 4:1 ratio,

$$F \times 4 \times 3 = 300 \times 9.81 \times 3$$

$$F = \frac{300 \times 9.81 \times 3}{4 \times 3}$$

$$= \underline{735.8\ N}$$

8.8 Exercises

1. (a) What is the difference between *mass* and *weight*?

(b) The force required to lift an electric cooker is 250 N, what is the mass of the cooker?

2.

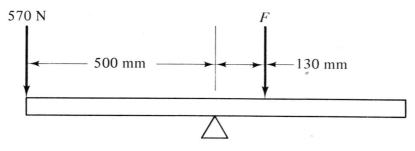

Fig. 8.8

By the principle of moments determine the force required (*F*) to maintain the bar of Fig. 8.8 in a horizontal position.

3. (a) Explain the underlying principle of tools and machines designed to raise loads with the minimum effort.

(b) State what kinds of losses could be expected to effect the machinery.

4. By means of an inclined plane, a bundle of conduit of mass 50 kg is hauled 20 m. If the conduit is raised to a vertical height of 5 m, calculate the force required for the operation assuming an efficiency of 55 per cent.

5. A screw jack has a pitch of 8 mm and a force of 200 N is exerted at the end of the arm of length 45 mm. What is the maximum load which can be raised by one revolution of the arm: (a) neglecting losses (b) with an efficiency of 66 per cent?

6. Draw a fully labelled sketch of a typical arrangement for a screw jack.

Examination and assignment hints

The following hints are given so that you can make the most of your educational and job-assignment efforts. However, success depends on the assimilation and consolidation of previous work as contained in this book and in your studies.

1. Successful numerical work requires: (a) neatness, (b) correctness, (c) speed, in the order given.

2. Before answering it is essential to study the question or assignment most carefully. Incorrect working will result if the question is not properly understood.

3. Whenever possible, change wording of the problem into an appropriate ruled sketch or circuit diagram and insert all values given.

4. It may be necessary to make rough checks. For this purpose do not use odd scraps of paper, but neatly show all working in a margin.

5. When you have difficulty in answering, don't panic. Try to visualize how the problem or assignment relates to a similar problem you have been engaged in, or start on a fresh question. Often when returning to the unanswered question you will find the solution.

6. Answers require an orderly arrangement showing a logical sequence – study the worked solutions contained in this book. Neatness is achieved by placing the equal signs vertically below each other.

7. For answers, most numbers require to be followed by units – otherwise they may be meaningless, e.g., 10 V, not simply 10.

8. Calculations require consistent units. For resistivity, if the length is in metres, the cross-sectional area must be in m^2. Where length is in mm, c.s.a in mm^2.

9. Be on your guard against 'distractors' as put in multiple-choice questions. As an example: 10 mV is given by

(a) $\frac{1}{10}$V   (b) $\frac{1}{100}$V

(c) 0.1 V   (d) 0.001 V

((b) is the correct answer.)

10. *Allow time for checking* as this may make all the difference between failure or a pass.

Answers to exercises

Chapter 1 (p. 15)

1. (a) $2\frac{47}{120}$ (b) $\frac{17}{24}$ (c) (i) 0.875 (ii) $\frac{52}{125}$
2. (a) 10 000 000 (b) 100 (c) 10^{10} (d) 10^6 (e) 16
3. (a) $\frac{y}{2}$ (b) $2y$ (c) $\sqrt{y}$ (d) y^2 (e) $y-2$ (f) $\frac{y}{2}+1$
   (g) y^2-a (h) $\sqrt{y-9}$
4. (a) 28.4 mm 32 mm
   (b) 500 μ V
5. (a) 12 (b) 54
6. (a) 0.00 108 m³ (b) 9.64 kg
7. 42.55 litres
8. £74.52
9. (b) 4 times greater
10. (b) (i) 1.76 mm (ii) 28 A

Chapter 2 (p. 31)

1. (a) 1.8 C (b) 960 Ω (c) (i) 2.4 kWh (ii) 6p
2. (a) 0.417 A, 0.625 A (b) 0.25 A, 144 V, 96 V
3. (a) 700 W (b) 87.5 W (c) 350 W
4. A-32 Ω B-53.3 Ω
5. (a) 60 A (b) 28p
6. (a) 100 Ω (b) 2 A (c) 100 V (d) 80 W (e) 400 W
7. (a) 3 A (b) A-83.3 Ω B-25 Ω (c) 2.5 kW (d) 13 A
8. 0.153 Ω
10. (b) (i) 5 A (ii) 48 Ω (iii) 1.2 kW (iv) 24p

Chapter 3 (p. 46)

10. (a) 15.56 J (b) 348 V

Chapter 4 (p. 55)

4. 70 V
5. 0.015 Ω 6. 2495 Ω

Chapter 5 (p. 72)

1. (a) (i) 440 turns (ii) 2.29 A
2. (a) 2000 W (b) 10 A

3. 5 Ω   4. (b) 70 A
5. (b) 3.6 kW   6. (a) 12.8 A, 8.6 kW   (b) 36 A, 25.8 kW
7. b   8. c   9. c
10. c   11. b

Crossword (p. 74)

ACROSS	DOWN
1. Reversals	1. Reactance
4. A.C.	2. VA
5. Hertz	3. Power
7. kW	6. Zero
9. Transformer	8. Gap
11. Nor	10. Sine
13. Cycle	12. Law
15. Back	14. CC
	16. kA

Chapter 6 (p. 85)

4. (a) 6 A   (b) 14.1 V
5. 11 V   6. 2 V   7. 0.03 Ω   8. 81.8%

Chapter 7 (p. 93)

3. (a) 167 °F   (b) 24 °C
4. (a) 6.25 A   (b) 38.4 Ω   (c) 10.8 MJ
6. 3 min, 18 sec

Chapter 8 (p. 101)

1. (b) 25 kg   2. 2192 N   4. 223 N
5. (a) 721 kg   (b) 476 kg

Index

Printed in Great Britain by J. W. Arrowsmith Ltd., Bristol